Chari...

ASSEMBLIES
FOR SECONDARY SCHOOLS

JAN THOMPSON

Hodder & Stoughton
A MEMBER OF THE HODDER HEADLINE GROUP

Charities Aid Foundation (CAF)

CAF is to receive the author's royalties on this book. CAF is a major financial institution in the charity-world, serving some 150,000 donors and benefiting thousands of charities.

CAF provides the easy, tax-free way to support your favourite charities and to respond to everyday appeals, on sums of money of any size and without having to take out individual covenants to the different charities. It can improve the value of your giving by reclaiming the tax for you on everything you give.

Some people prefer CAF to distribute their charity for them, and it is therefore able to support a wide range of charities, as well as having a special disasters emergency fund to respond promptly in times of desperate need.

For more information contact:

Charities Aid Foundation
48 Pembury Road
Tonbridge, KENT TN9 2JD
Tel. 0732 771333

British Library Cataloguing in Publication Data

Thompson, Jan
    Charities: Assemblies for Secondary Schools
    I. Title
    377

ISBN 0-340-58796-2

First published 1993
Impression number 10 9 8 7 6 5 4 3 2 1
Year   1998 1997 1996 1995 1994 1993

Typeset by Rowland Phototypesetting Ltd, Bury St Edmunds, Suffolk.
Printed in Great Britain for Hodder & Stoughton Educational, a division of Hodder Headline PLC, Mill Road, Dunton Green, Sevenoaks, Kent TN13 2YA by Athenaeum Press Ltd, Newcastle upon Tyne.

Acknowledgements

The Publishers would like to thank the following for their kind permission to reproduce material:

Age Concern for extracts from their *Coming of Age Campaign Resources for Teachers*; Amnesty International for extracts from *What Does Amnesty International Do?* and other extracts from Amnesty leaflets; British Heart Foundation for extracts from BHF leaflets; The Children's Society for extracts from *Gateway* and the 'No Fooling' Campaign; Christian Aid for extracts from various leaflets and newsletters and *Youth Topics*; The Ellenor Foundation for extracts from *Our First Five Years* and *Hospice 'Casa Sperantei'* Issue No. 1, News '92; Friends of the Earth for extracts from *Earth Matters* and *Ozone Destruction*; Help the Aged for extracts from *Adopt a Granny*; Imperial Cancer Research for extract from *Conquest*; I.O.W. Donkey Sanctuary; Lepra for extracts from *Lepra Today* and *LEPRA News*; Marie Curie Cancer Care for extract from a letter to supporters; MIND for the extract from a newsletter, November 1991; Monkey World; Oxfam for extract from *Oxfam News*; RSPCA; The Salvation Army for extracts from *The Caring Touch* and *Despatches*; The Samaritans; Shelter for extracts from various leaflets, letters, mailings to supporters and *A Christmas Service on Homelessness and Housing*; Save the Children Fund for extracts from *Save the Children Review* 1992 and *World's Children* 1992; Sight Savers for extract from *Horizons* Autumn 1991; The Spastics Society for extracts from various leaflets and pamphlets; The Terrence Higgins Trust for extracts from leaflets and the newsletter from Martyn Taylor 1991; United Nations Association for the extract from *The Earth is in Environmental Crisis* and *Special Report*; UNICEF UK for the extract from Information Sheet 9; WaterAid for extracts from *Oasis*, The WaterAid Journal; Scripture taken from the HOLY BIBLE, NEW INTERNATIONAL VERSION. Copyright 1973, 1978, 1984 by International Bible Society. Used by permission. All rights reserved.

Every effort has been made to trace copyright holders of material reproduced in this book. The Publishers will be glad to make suitable arrangements with any copyright holders whom it has not been possible to contact.

CONTENTS

Introduction: Please read this!

Charities

This book is a resource to be used alongside any other contacts with charity groups that are available to your school; but it is structured in such a way that it can be used for school worship. It is not intended to be an alternative to direct involvement with charities, nor is it a substitute for visits to the school by their representatives; you are encouraged to contact the charities themselves for further information, materials, videos etc., (an address list is included on p. 131).

'Collective worship'

Charities provide popular themes for school assemblies, but in what sense are they 'collective worship'? Here is a ready source of material on British charities which goes beyond straight descriptions of their work, to draw out their underlying values and to encourage pupils to think about these for themselves.

Chapters

The material is presented in units suitable for individual acts of worship, which are collected into sections, most of which concentrate on a particular charity. They could, of course, be combined for longer assemblies, in which case you may wish to rearrange the material, putting the prayers together, for example.

'Of a broadly Christian character'

There is a sense in which all these acts of worship are 'of a broadly Christian character' because of the values which they encourage pupils to reflect upon. But, while some have more explicit Christian content where this is appropriate to the charities concerned, all the themes are appropriate to pupils, whatever their religious or secular background.

Posters

Sometimes the theme is a slogan, like 'For God's sake, care'. You could have posters made of the slogan and post them round the school beforehand. On the morning of the assembly, have them posted in the hall. In some cases, suitable posters may be obtained from the charities concerned. Similarly, if the assemblies for several consecutive days are about the same charity, it would be worth having posters or a large banner in the hall with the name and logo of the charity.

Readers

Although it is possible for these acts of worship to be led by one person, it is preferable to have a number of readers. The material is set out in short sections to facilitate this and should only require the minimum preparation time. Try experimenting with voices from different parts of the school hall or from different raised positions on the school stage. Suggestions are given (in italics) at the beginning of each assembly; sometimes it is recommended that adults or senior pupils should read because of the nature of the material or its difficult vocabulary.

Role-play

Try, where possible, to use role-play. If passages from a diary are being used, the reader could be seated at a table pretending to write the diary as he reads. A story could be told with the reader out of view, using a microphone, with the story being enacted on the stage. Some passages could be read by someone dressed appropriately for the part. Questions and answers might be presented with an interviewer asking the questions of another person. Again, suggestions are given (in italics) at the beginning of the acts of worship.

Question and answer

Sometimes there are questions in the text. You may treat these as rhetorical questions and give the answers fairly quickly. Or, with a smaller assembly in a more informal setting, you may wish to see what answers the pupils can suggest.

Anecdotes

Sometimes there are references to our own experiences (e.g. 'Those of us who wear glasses know what it is like to see things out of focus'). These could be developed by a teacher who has the confidence to break off from reading and just talk in a 'chatty' way about a relevant real-life situation, particularly if it is amusing.

Prayers

Set prayers are given for those who want them. You should introduce the prayers in ways which are appropriate to your own situation. Some people prefer to invite pupils to listen to the prayer and make it their own if they wish, rather than assuming that all pupils can be involved in 'Let us pray'. The prayers are addressed to 'Lord' so that they could be used by believers from any religious tradition.

Often the prayers are in the form of meditations requiring time for pupils to pursue their own thoughts. It is quite a skill to estimate how much time to allow: it must be enough to be worthwhile, but not so much that pupils get fidgety and wonder what is happening. The use of silence in acts of worship is something which many schools are now taking seriously, but it is a skill which needs to be taught and practised, beginning with just a very short period of silence and gradually extending it.

Credits

Most of this material has been taken from newsletters, magazines and leaflets produced by the various charities represented here. We are grateful for their kind permission to use and reproduce it.

AGE CONCERN

1 Ageism

Use at least two readers, taking alternative paragraphs.

We've all heard of racism and sexism – discrimination against people because of their race or sex – and now there is a new word: ageism. The *word* may be new, but Age Concern was championing the rights of older people half a century ago and over the last 50 years it has been helping them to lead happy and fulfilling lives.

Age Concern began in 1940 during the Second World War when many older people were evacuated from their homes for safety, and isolated from their families. In its early years this charity was called the National Old People's Welfare Committee, and it brought together all the major agencies working for the good of older people.

At the beginning of this century, fewer than 1 in 20 people were over 65, and only 1 in 500 was over 85. That has now changed. One in every 8 people is over 65, and 1 in a 100 is over 85. Forecasters suggest that by the early twenty-first century 1 in 50 or more people will be over 85! By the year 2025 nearly a quarter of the population will be over retirement age, and most adults in Britain will be over 50. This is because we are having fewer children and better health care means that more people are living into old age.

Age Concern is the largest charity in Britain providing services for elderly people. 1990 was its Golden Jubilee Year and today there are over 1,400 Age Concern organisations in the UK. These are run by over 250,000 volunteers. They may drive people to and from hospital, organise activities in a day centre, or serve in their charity shop. Behind the scenes they may be doing secretarial work or organising fund raising events.

Each local Age Concern group decides what is most important for the older people in its own community. Some compile a directory of all the local resources for retired people in the area. Most offer advice to the retired on financial matters – explaining about pensions and other benefits.

Age Concern England – the central body – publishes books such as *Living, loving and ageing* and *Life in the Sun – A guide to long-stay holidays and living abroad in retirement*. There are also many factsheets available on a wide range of issues, such as health care.

Many of the Age Concern groups are run by older people themselves. They have many skills that they can share, and more time to devote to the work. Most retired people in their 60s do not consider themselves old and they want to help others who are older than themselves.

Age Concern groups encourage their members to take up new hobbies. These include learning to play a musical instrument or speak a foreign language, calligraphy, computing and swimming. One Agewell project in Hammersmith had five pensioners absailing down the 40 metre high tower of the Town Hall, to prove that older people can rise to new challenges!

Prayer

When we are little, we want to be older. A child doesn't say 'I'm seven', but 'I'm seven-and-a-half' or 'Seven-and-three-quarters'. They are always looking forward to being a year older. In the same way, teenagers want to be grown up.

Yet you/we regard 30-year olds as middle aged, 40-year olds as over the hill, and 50-year olds as 'wrinklies'. But as people grow old, the 30 and 40 year olds seem positively young. And do people really feel very different as the decades pass? Aren't they still essentially the same people, whatever they look like on the outside? And aren't we as young as we feel?

Dear Lord, help us not to judge people by their ages – to dismiss them as too young or too old. Help us to accept people whatever their age and to value them for what they are.

Amen

2 The times they are a-changing

*Seek the help of your Drama Department in presenting the timeline.
Divide up the rest of the paragraphs between a number of readers, with a
different voice asking the questions, printed in bold type, to those reading
the answers.*

Vera Smith's timeline:

1900   Vera was born, in the same year as the Queen Mother.

1901   Queen Victoria dies.
Invention of the vacuum cleaner.

1907   Electric kettles still a novelty.
Invention of the first electric washing machine.

1909   First old age pensions available.

1914   Vera leaves school, aged 14.

1914–1918 World War I.
Vera's father and oldest brother were killed in active service.

1921   Vera marries and has 4 children. But the war has affected the
number of available marriage partners for women and many do
not find husbands.

1934   Unemployment figures running at 17% after the worst of the
Great Depression.

1938   Mr. Biro invents the ballpoint pen.

1939–1945 World War II.
Vera's home is bombed and she is evacuated.

1948   National Health Service established.

1960   Vera reaches retirement age.
Consumer boom. Jet airlines.

1965   Vera's husband retires.

1967   92% of the population own TV sets (black and white).

1969   First moon landing.

1971	Pocket calculators available in the shops.
1972	Inflation hits savings and fixed pensions. Vera's husband dies.
1980s	Vera lives alone, suffers slightly from arthritis but remains largely independent and hopes to stay this way for as long as possible.
1986	Vera goes to live in an old person's flat where there is a warden on call.
1990	Vera died. 'Much loved mother, grandmother and great grandmother.'

(From 'Time Line', part of Age Concern of England's 'Coming of Age Campaign Resources for Teachers')

One person in every hundred in Britain is over 85. Like Vera, they have lived through two World Wars, with all the personal suffering and social upheaval that these entail, and seen miraculous technological changes.

Life for them has been an experience of loss and change. But life for all of us is loss and change, however long or short a life we live. In fact, there is usually far more adjustment to make in the first third of our lives than in all the rest. This means that young people can often have a very good understanding of the fears and bewilderment of some elderly people.

What is meant by loss and change?

In Vera Smith's case there was the loss of hundreds of thousands of British forces in the First World War, among whom were her father and oldest brother. In the Second World War she lost her home. When she was 72 her husband died and she was left to face another 18 years of life on her own. Apart from these personal changes to her life and circumstances, there were amazing changes going on around her as she lived through each successive decade of the twentieth century. Life in the 1980s was a far cry from life when Vera was born, before the age of airtravel, television or microcomputers.

And what does loss and change mean for young people today?

There is the loss of security when a toddler leaves his parents for the first time to stay at a play group.

4

There is the loss of individual attention when you go to school.

Perhaps the loss of a dearly loved pet.

The loss of some of your class-mates when you change to secondary school.

The loss of a grandparent, perhaps.

The loss of self-confidence in a subject you find difficult or a failed exam.

Changes come thick and fast as you meet new experiences, new people, new skills.

Loss brings with it much personal suffering, but the changes it forces upon us can bring new opportunities which are challenging and exciting as well as somewhat frightening.

Older people have been through all this and much more. They know that they managed to cope with many things that were frightening at the time. They know that time heals sorrows which they once thought they would never get over.

Young people, on the other hand, have energy and time on their side. You know that if you make mistakes, you have time to try again.

Prayer

Dear Lord, we all experience loss and change.
Please give us the strength to cope with situations that frighten us.
Help us to be more understanding of the feelings of others, both young and old, who are also experiencing loss and change.

Amen

HELP THE AGED

1 In the UK

Display the Help the Aged logo
Use different voices for the starred paragraphs. These readers could be
positioned around the hall.

1991 saw the 30th anniversary of Help the Aged, a charity which exists to
meet the needs of frail, isolated and poor elderly people. Its fund raising
enables it to carry on programmes to help older people and to promote
better awareness and understanding of their needs among the general
public.

What are the needs of elderly people?

★ They want to be able to continue to live for as long as possible in their
own homes; but elderly people on their own are afraid that if they fall
down, no-one will know that they need help. So Help the Aged fits
community alarms so that elderly people can call for help.

★ They need to keep warm in winter. So Help the Aged runs a Winter
Warmth Line with help and simple advice on how to keep out the winter
cold.

★ They need decent housing. So Help the Aged runs some sheltered accommodation specially built for elderly people where they can live independently but with a warden on hand. They also manage many properties which have been donated to them for elderly people.

★ Older people want to continue being able to get around, even though they may be too frail to drive or too poor to run a car. So Help the Aged provides vehicles for community transport, so that elderly people can be given lifts to the shops and other places.

★ They want to have friends to talk to, after their own partners have died. So Help the Aged supports day centres where elderly people can meet together.

★ They want to be well fed, even though they may not feel like going to the trouble of cooking for one. So Help the Aged supports luncheon clubs where older people can get a hot meal.

★ They want to stay fit. Old age is not an illness and older people should be able to continue to enjoy good health. So Help the Aged supports research into the prevention of chronic disabling illnesses which affect elderly people.

★ Eventually, when they get too frail to look after themselves, elderly people need to be cared for with dignity. Help the Aged runs four residential homes for this purpose.

Prayer

The logo for Help the Aged is a rising sun, to remind us that older people still have lives worth living and hopes for the future. In many societies, older people are valued for their wisdom and experience of life; and as their bodies grow frail, they are cared for within their families and communities. Help us, Lord, to respect elderly people; and thank you for charities like Help the Aged which give older people new hope for tomorrow.

Amen

2   Adopt a granny

Display the logo. Use a variety of readers. A different voice could be used for each of the four sections of the newspaper advertisement, with the four speakers reading their passages out from newspapers.

Help the Aged not only works for elderly people in Britain, but it is the only UK charity which addresses the needs specifically of elderly people abroad – in Africa, Asia, Latin America and the Caribbean. One way in which it helps is through its 'Adopt a granny' scheme. This is how the scheme is described in an advert in a Sunday paper:

Why sponsor a Granny?

For many elderly people in the world's poorest countries, old age is a time to dread, especially if they have no family to look after them. That's why we started Adopt a granny – the only UK based sponsorship scheme that aims to help elderly people.

Change a life

Nang Chin, a widow, is one 'granny' whose life has been changed by her UK sponsors. Frail and destitute, she was once terrified of what would become of her. Now she has the basic things she needs – food, clothing and medicine. Above all, hope and self-respect.

Help a community

By sponsoring someone like Nang, you will help more than one elderly person. Part of your contribution will help local communities improve the lives of elderly people.

Less than £2 a week

It doesn't cost much to sponsor a granny. To find out how much your support can mean, clip the coupon now and post it to Help the Aged.

An interesting part of this scheme is that it helps individual 'grannys' and also provides money for projects to help raise the living standards of whole communities where elderly people live. So it doesn't just pick out individuals at the expense of the majority.

Over 12,000 grannies and grandads are now being sponsored by families and individuals in the UK and Europe. They have found that this practical, personal way of helping elderly people has brought them great satisfaction and joy, as they bring hope and security into the lives of poor and anxious people.

8

For David Jeffcock, the greatest experience of his life came when he visited his 'Gran', Rosemary, in Kenya in 1991.

David recalls his astonishment on finding the whole village had turned out to greet him. But despite the crowds, he soon recognised the smiling face of Rosemary.

She took him to see her home and small vegetable plot, whilst she chatted excitedly to him through an interpreter.

David soon realised how much his three years of friendship and support had meant to Rosemary as she explained about the medicines, food and clothing it had allowed her to buy. She also told him that his help had enabled her to grow her own vegetables on the neatly kept plot of land.

David's most lasting memory of the trip though was the joy on Rosemary's face when they met. It's something he'll never forget.

Says David, 'Rosemary lives a simple life and wants nothing else. But the help I can give her means she can enjoy an acceptable living standard. Without it I can see she'd be living in poverty.'
(Leaflet about Adopt a Granny, Help the Aged)

Prayer

We shouldn't really need it, but there is a satisfaction in knowing where our money is going when we give to charity. A satisfaction in having a name and a photograph and some details about the person we are helping. There is a similar appeal when we see the faces of individuals on television on those occasions when we are alerted to some tragedy in the world. We pray that these faces will become for us symbols of the faceless millions who suffer and who need our compassion just as much.

Amen

BRITISH HEART FOUNDATION

British Heart Foundation
The heart research charity

1   Take heart

You could display the British Heart Foundation logo (above). Use different readers for each of the starred paragraphs.

Heart disease claims a life every two minutes. That makes it Britain's biggest killer. While it is true that this mainly affects older people, 5,000 children are born each year with hearts that do not work properly. People who are living with heart disease can find that just getting through each day can be a tremendous effort.

The British Heart Foundation is the main charity in the field of heart disease. It began in 1961. By the end of the 1960s its income was about half a million pounds a year. By the end of the 1980s this figure had risen to 29 million pounds. This money is put to good use, covering four areas of work:

★ First and foremost the British Heart Foundation funds research. Only through research can doctors hope to understand more about the causes, treatment and ways of preventing heart disease. Many thousands of men, women and children today owe their lives to the progress made through research. For instance, every patient who undergoes heart surgery goes on a heart–lung machine which was developed from research funded by the BHF.

★ BHF also provides equipment and training to help the medical services cope with heart disease. In recent years it has helped to equip ambulances with defibrillators. The first hour after a patient has suffered a heart attack is critical, so the work of the ambulance crew is vital. With this machinery, they can give an electric shock to try to restore the normal rhythm of the heart, without waiting to get the patient to hospital for this treatment. Thousands of lives are being saved in this way.

★ Money is also spent on helping patients return to a full and active life after heart attacks or surgery. BHF funds rehabilitation programmes in hospitals and ex-patients' heart support groups.

★ It also runs an education programme, producing eye-catching posters and free booklets aimed at the general public and young people in particular. Each year it sends a newsletter to all schools with 12–13 year old pupils, with latest information about things like the effect of diet and exercise on our hearts. It has produced a video for the general public called 'Don't just stand there!', with advice on what to do when someone has a heart attack. It also produces reports to keep doctors up to date with their latest research findings.

The British Heart Foundation's newsletter is called *Take Heart*, and there is much to take heart about in the development of knowledge about heart disease and its treatment. Only recently 750 heart transplant patients took part in the 14th annual British Transplant Games, showing that heart transplant patients can be fit, healthy athletes. Heart surgery has come an amazingly long way since 1961 when the British Heart Foundation was first established.

Prayer

Many of us have friends and relatives – perhaps grandparents – who have died from heart attacks or other forms of heart disease. Or perhaps we know someone suffering from a heart condition. If so, spend a few moments thinking about them now, giving thanks for all that they mean to you.

Amen

2   Case studies

Display the British Heart Foundation logo (see p. 10).
Use a different reader for each case study. The third reader should also say the prayer.

The following three people have benefited from the research of the British Heart Foundation.

★ When Karen was born in November 1988, she seemed to be a normal, healthy baby. But at five weeks old her parents were very worried because she wasn't putting on weight, as she should. She was admitted to a local hospital, where serious heart defects were discovered. The following morning, Karen was rushed by ambulance to the John Radcliffe Hospital in Oxford, where she underwent surgery that saved her life with only hours to spare.

Karen had another major heart operation in those early months of her life, but she is now at nursery school with her friends, and even attends gym and dancing classes – with great enthusiasm. Research on the heart conditions that affect children has progressed so far that Karen, and thousands of children like her, are now fit and well, and leading normal lives.

★ George left work one day feeling slightly unwell. Within minutes of arriving home, he suffered a massive coronary, followed ten days later by a severe stroke. He was 32.

After six weeks in hospital, George returned home, but he was still in constant pain. Over the next few years, George had no less than *seven* heart attacks, and was so weak that he spent 18 months in a wheelchair and six months in hospital. His condition was so bad that, at first, doctors thought a heart transplant wouldn't help him. But after more extensive tests, George was eventually given a new heart in a transplant operation carried out by Professor Sir Magdi Yacoub, a famous pioneering transplant surgeon. The operation was a success and George is now alive and well – with a new baby son to keep him and his wife busy.

(Both case studies taken from the leaflet 'You can help BHF save lives through a legacy')

★ Another person who has benefited from heart surgery is John. In a way, he is quite a celebrity now, because his was the very first heart operation to be shown live on television. It was part of *Hospital Watch* on BBC TV in September 1991. A little after the operation, John said this:

I'd never been in hospital before, so I was nervous. I'm only 47, and I began to think that I wouldn't live to enjoy my retirement. Professor Taylor said he needed to replace my aortic valve immediately, to give me a better chance. By now, I was really apprehensive. But one of the nurses gave me some leaflets from the British Heart Foundation – they really put my mind at rest by explaining everything in layman's terms.

My operation went really well – I was out of hospital after 8 days. I had so many letters and cards from well wishers after *Hospital Watch* – one bloke even said it gave his wife the courage to have the same operation. I'm still taking it easy, but I'm hoping to get back to work in the New Year. I'm even looking forward to playing a bit of football.
(*BHF leaflet, 1991*)

Prayer

We give thanks for the caring communities in which we live – for the general public who are moved to send their good wishes to strangers they see or hear about on TV. It is often said that television can dull our senses by showing so much misery and violence that we either take it for granted, or shut it out because we cannot take in any more; but television can also make us aware of people – real people like you and me – who are in need, and can move us to do something to help them. We pray that our own hearts will never be cold or hardened to the needs of others.

Amen

SHELTER

1   How it began

This would be best read by an adult.

This was written in 1991 by Cardinal Hume, the President of Shelter:

Twenty five years ago, the BBC showed a documentary about one of the greatest social evils of our time. It caused an outcry from the public such as had never been seen before. Indeed, it even led to a special cabinet meeting. The documentary was 'Cathy Come Home' and its subject matter was the then 'new' problem of homelessness.

Sadly today homelessness is still with us and familiar to us all. Yet in the sixties, Cathy's story was the first time many people had ever thought about homelessness – and they were horrified.

The documentary – based on the real experiences of homeless people – tells the moving story of Cathy and Reg and their struggle to find a home. Unable to keep up with the rent when Reg loses his job, the couple are shunted from one temporary place to another. Eventually Cathy has no choice but to take her children to a hostel for homeless women where husbands aren't allowed. When her statutory six months stay is up, viewers witness a heartbreaking closing scene in which her children are taken away and put 'in care'.

The viewers, watching in a decade when they'd been told they'd 'never had it so good', simply couldn't believe that in a wealthy country like Britain there was nowhere for homeless people like Cathy and Reg to turn for help.

It was for this reason that Shelter was set up.

I remember quite clearly the coming together of church and charitable housing trusts around the country in 1967 to form Shelter.

Today, as Shelter's President, I am glad to be associated with a movement which, over the last 25 years, has constantly campaigned for homeless people to find accommodation.

Only recently I heard about a couple whose story is almost identical to that told in 'Cathy Come Home'. The family, Ian and Susan and their baby boy, found themselves homeless when the caravan they had been living in became uninhabitable and they had to leave. When Shelter first heard about them, Ian had just lost his job and was sleeping in their car and Susan and the baby were staying with a friend in the living room.

Thankfully I am pleased to tell you that, unlike Cathy's story, this one does have a happy ending. Thanks to Shelter workers in Susan's area, the Council agreed to house the family together.

Yet while it is fortunate that charities like Shelter are here to help people like Ian and Susan, it is also distressing that in a wealthy society like ours homelessness should still be on the increase. Official figures show that there are more homeless people in Britain today than ever before: in 1966 more than 13,000 people were homeless – today the figure is near 420,000.
(Letter of November 1991 from Cardinal Hume to Shelter supporters)

It is because of the continuing rise in homelessness that Shelter launched its most important campaign, in its 25th Anniversary Year. A detailed report called 'Building for the Future' was presented in the House of Commons, inviting MPs to discuss Shelter's proposals to achieve adequate and decent housing for all before the end of the century.

Prayer

As Shelter works closely with the Churches, the following is a Christian prayer for homeless people:

Loving God,
You came through Jesus to share our life,
You made your home among the poor,
You made yourself one with all people everywhere.
Hear our prayers for all who are homeless and badly housed.
May we too listen to their voices and respond in faith.

Amen

(From Shelter's 'A Christmas Service on Homelessness and Housing')

2 Home truths

*One main narrator should read out the starred sentences, while six other readers should each take one of the statements in direct speech.
All seven readers could join together in the final statement about Shelter.
A new reader should take the prayers.*

★ Shelter estimates that there are currently 3 million people in Britain without their own homes. There has been a 30 per cent increase in official homelessness in England since 1987. Between 1980 and 1989 only one council house was built for every three council houses sold.

'My husband is so down, he doesn't know what to do. He can't find a job, and it's been so long now no-one wants to know. What will we do? The council says we are intentionally homeless. They won't even put us in bed-and-breakfast.'

★ The use of shortlife and privately leased accommodation has continued to increase . . . At the same time the provision of permanent local authority housing has declined.

'Polly asked me why she couldn't play like other children – why she always has to be quiet and never run about. How can I tell her I'm afraid of being kicked out of this awful place?'

★ There are about 8,000 people sleeping rough in England.

'He said I must *like* sleeping rough or I wouldn't do it. How would *he* like it, being cold and wet and dirty all the time? It makes you want to hit out at people, when you hear that stuff.'

★ Over 80 per cent of London's homeless young people came to the capital to look for work. The charity, Centrepoint, estimates that there are 50,000 young homeless people in central London between the ages of 16 and 19.

'I know my Dad'll thump me again if I stick around, so I'd better go. But I don't know where to go. My mates don't have any space. And anyway some of them are on drugs. I don't want to start *that*.'

★ The mental health charity, MIND, estimates that there are 3,000 homeless people in London with mental health problems. Other vulnerable groups which are over represented among the homeless are black people and women.

'I don't know – I wanted to come out of that hospital – but it's all so confusing. They *said* I could cope, but no one came to see me and I forgot everything they told me and didn't pay the rent. So I was turned out. What'll I do now?'

★ In England 835,000 disabled people are living in accommodation unsuited to their needs.

'I used to love this place, but now I can't afford to heat it. The stairs are a problem too, so I sleep on a bed in the living room.'

Shelter believes that a decent affordable home should be available to everybody as a basic human right.

(Most of this material is taken from service sheets and statistics issued by Shelter in 1991)

Prayer

We pray for those who have no home of their own:
– nowhere to be warm and comfortable,
– nowhere to relax,
– nowhere to wash and cook,
– nowhere for the children to play,
– nowhere to keep their possessions safe,
– nowhere special of their own,
– nowhere to invite their friends,
– nowhere to feel secure,
– nowhere to call their own.
Help us, Lord, who have so much, never to look down on homeless people.

Amen

3 Case study: a young family

For dramatic effect, the first reader (Mary) should be seated at an office desk. She opens the letter and begins to read it out loud. The second reader (Tania) should be seated in a chair, and pretends to write the letter as she reads it out from the second paragraph onwards.
At the end of the letter, Mary picks up her chair and goes and sits with Tania while a third reader finishes the story.

Dear Shelter,

I am writing to you in the hope that you might be able to help me and my husband find somewhere to live. I've heard on the TV how you stand up for the rights of homeless people, and wondered if you could help us.

. . .

Basically everything started to go wrong when my husband lost his job at his factory. We got behind in our mortgage repayments and lost our house. Since then me and my 3-year-old son Martin have been staying at my sister's, and my husband Dave is living in a bedsit.

It's not up to much but it's better than nothing, and I suppose at least he's not walking the streets. The main problem is that the place he's renting is miles away from my sister's house and so it's like being separated. We're both so depressed these days that when we do get together we end up taking it out on each other and it's tearing us apart.

Sometimes I think about the time when we'd just had Martin. I had so many plans for us all then. Now we're hardly together, and Martin is just too young to understand why we can't live with his Daddy anymore.

It doesn't seem two minutes ago that I sat in the lounge of our house watching a programme on TV about families being thrown out of their homes. Then, homelessness was something that happened to 'other people' who'd tried to buy houses they couldn't afford. But we thought we were buying within our means, and now it's happening to us!

I remember our marriage vows about staying together for better for worse, for richer for poorer and all that, but I just don't know if I can take any more of this.

That's why I am writing to you. If only we could be together again as a family, I know we'd be able to sort out our problems and get ourselves back on our feet.

Yours faithfully
Tania Robbins

Mary spent time talking to Tania, assessed the situation and started work on finding them a home. Like all our staff, she has been trained by Shelter in housing law, as well as counselling. So she knows about people's rights to housing, what benefits they are entitled to – and most importantly, *where* housing vacancies may arise.

And because people like Mary work in the heart of the community, they build a network of contacts – including the Council, local landlords, solicitors and Housing Associations.

So, after lengthy negotiations, the Council agreed to house Dave, Tania and Martin in permanent accommodation.

(From a letter to Shelter published in a mailing to supporters 1991)

Prayer

We pray for homeless people and the badly housed and for all who try to serve them – for those who work in shelters, housing departments and advice centres, and for the efforts of tenants associations. In particular, we pray for the charity, Shelter.

Amen

4 Case study: the single homeless

There are three main sections here which could be taken by three different readers.

On the site of an old warehouse near the town centre sits an old car. This is where Bill has spent most nights for the past two years. Someone has taken the wheels for spares, most of the windows are broken, but Bill huddles up on the back seat which has survived intact. The car is a good find. Away from the main streets, he can avoid the stares of evening theatre-goers, and the insults from those queueing to get into the busy night clubs.

Life hasn't always been like this for Bill. In his mid-twenties Bill led a team of construction workers who travelled all over Britain to work on various building projects. In the 60s they secured work on the M1 motorway project. Later, in the 70s, they helped build hundreds of new homes in the expanding suburbs of North London.

Bill's lifestyle revolved around his work. But as he grew older, his work became too strenuous. He tried to get office jobs, but he had no experience and they only seemed to want younger candidates.

Bill was caught in a downward spiral that he felt powerless to stop. With no job, no-one wanted to give him lodgings. Without lodgings, he had to sleep rough, and on the streets it was difficult to find a place to shave and wash. Even old friends didn't want to know him. Bill's health is growing worse every day – and gangrene now threatens the amputation of his left leg. It is no wonder he feels shunned by society.

One Christmas Eve, Bill found it too bitterly cold to sleep out, so he slept in a bus – but was 'moved on' by the police.

When Bill came to one of Shelter's Housing Aid Centres, we were appalled that a man in his state of health was sleeping out. Yet due to the severe shortage of suitable housing in the area, it took us weeks of patient phone calls to help find Bill a small, unfurnished council flat. The flat is on the first floor, so Bill may find the stairs difficult – but at least he has the warmth and security of a place he can call 'home'.
(Taken from a Shelter leaflet)

There are many single homeless people like Bill who sleep rough on our streets, while we're tucked up in a warm bed. Shelter estimates that there are up to 3,000 people sleeping rough each night in London and a further 5,000 in the rest of England. Many more live on the streets in the daytime but find shelter in hostels at night.

February 1991 saw some of the coldest weather in Britain for several years. Strong north-easterly winds brought sub-zero temperatures, and many towns lay under a thick blanket of snow. Within two days Shelter had arranged 50 emergency night shelters around the country. This was achieved with the help of local voluntary groups, churches and Shelter staff. It was followed up by contacting local MPs and with a report to government.

The long-term result of that February crisis is Shelter Nightline – a new emergency telephone service, run from the Shelter headquarters in London, to help people who find themselves out on the streets at night with nowhere to go. Each afternoon a precise record is made of all the spare emergency beds in London. This is put onto the Nightline computer system, ready to help the many desperate people who phone in at night, when other agencies are closed. The information on the computer is revised throughout the night as beds are filled. This service is proving very popular, particularly when the cold weather begins to bite.

Prayer

We pray for people like Bill whose hopes in life have been shattered, who have been caught in a downward spiral with no-one to help them stop, and have hit rock bottom.
People who despair of ever finding life worthwhile again.
People who once had jobs, money, homes, relationships,
whose world has fallen apart around them.
'Lord of all hopefulness' who has given us resilience and resourcefulness,
bless those who strengthen the weak,
who lift up the downhearted,
and give hope to the despairing.

Amen

5   Case study: young people

Write up LEAP in large letters and what it stands for.
You will need two readers – the first could also say the prayer.

All too often, young people find that their chances of getting a job are decided not by their skills and abilities but by whether they have a home. Employers tend not to hire homeless people, which in turn gives them little chance of securing a place to live.

LEAP – the Linked Employment and Accommodation Project – which Shelter helped to set up in South London, is breaking this vicious cycle of homelessness and joblessness.

LEAP is run by Shelter, the Industrial Society and several interested employers. It offers homeless and jobless young people a two week course which helps them to succeed in interviews, as well as, preparing them for the type of work involved. The trainees are guaranteed an interview at the end of the course; and it is Shelter's role to find them somewhere affordable to live.

A year after its launch, 30 young people have succeeded on the course, found a home and been offered a job. Building on the success of the London LEAP, Shelter is starting a new scheme in Bristol.

Peter is one of those 30 people:

Previously he had learned not to mention the hostel where he was staying when he went for job interviews. His voluntary work leading a youth group counted in his favour, but as he said 'employers think people in hostels are all the same – as if we were all on drugs or had a drinking problem'.

After the LEAP course, he had an interview with the Body Shop who saw the main things about Peter – that he was very keen to get back to work and that he was very sharp.

The training course and chance of a job had come at a vital time for Peter, catching him when his confidence was fading. But once in the job, Peter went through a tough time. The hostel was too noisy and he really needed a place to be on his own and relax when he finished work. Spending all day on his feet in the shop was much more exhausting than he had imagined.

22

But he kept going, with support at this workplace and contact with Shelter's LEAP worker. Within a couple of months he found a place to live through a Housing Association. It needed a lot of painting and decorating, and the rent was quite high for him, but he felt he was ready to take it on. LEAP gave him a grant of £150 to help towards the furnishings.

This is one example of how Shelter is helping homeless young people to make their own way in life.

(Taken and adapted from 'Homes for today, hope for tomorrow' – a Shelter leaflet, 1991)

Prayer

Starting out on adult life is exciting and challenging and sometimes also a bit confusing and frightening. What must it be like for youngsters without families to back them up and without homes to come back to?

There are times when we long for independence and for our own space – but let us also be thankful for those who care for us and stand by us as we grow up and start to make our own way in life.

Amen

THE SALVATION ARMY

1   An army without guns

The Salvation Army slogan 'For God's sake, care' could be put up on display for this assembly. The passage falls into sections for a number of readers.

The Salvation Army is a branch of the Christian Church which goes back to 1865 and the work of William Booth on the streets of the East End of London. In 1878 the Christian Mission that he started was reorganised on a military basis and given the title 'The Salvation Army', with William Booth as its first General. As an 'army', it is very efficiently run. Its committed members are called soldiers and they wear uniform when involved with Salvation Army work. Its full-time, ordained ministers, both men and women, are officers who wear uniform all the time. They may hold the rank of lieutenant, captain, colonel, major or commissioner, with the one General in overall command. These uniformed Salvationists accept a life of disciplined self-denial and obedience to their superior officers, and they speak about their 'years of service'. They worship in places called 'Citadels', have a newspaper called *The War Cry*, and send out 'Despatches' to their supporters with 'News from the front'.

But this is no ordinary army. This army fights, not with guns, but with the power of love. The purpose of the *Salvation* Army is not to kill, but to help people lead fuller lives. It believes that fulfilment can only be found in Jesus Christ, but it also recognises that people cannot listen to the Gospel when they are cold, or hungry, or sleeping rough, or hooked on drugs, or isolated, or depressed, or in the midst of a crisis or disaster. So the Salvation Army goes out into the community and lives out the Gospel in action wherever it is needed.

Salvationists work with children and the elderly. Their hostels shelter the single homeless, and their Goodwill Centres are places where lonely people can find friendship and help with their domestic problems. They have rehabilitation centres to help people fight drug addiction and drunkenness. They run a Family Tracing Service to find lost relatives and friends. Whenever a disaster strikes, like a major train or aeroplane accident, the Salvation Army is there offering refreshments to the emergency teams and comfort to the survivors. They visit people in prisons, and offer them support when they come out. Not only do they work in Britain, but in many countries throughout the world the Salvation Army uniform is recognised, trusted and respected.

So next time you see the Salvation Army out on the streets with their brass bands and collecting boxes, think about their commitment, their care for all who suffer misfortune, and remember this slogan of theirs:

For God's sake, care.

Prayer

The Salvation Army asks for commitment from its members and sets itself high standards – those of Jesus Christ himself. Whether we would call ourselves Christians, or followers of other religions, or whatever our beliefs – let us think for a moment what difference our beliefs make to our lives. Do we believe in helping others? And are our beliefs important enough for us to do something about them?

Amen

2   We're all going on a summer holiday

Use a number of readers for this.

Holidays have come to dominate many people's lives. We plan and talk about where we are going, and it remains a topic of conversation for weeks after we've got back. Holiday programmes on television, tempting us with exotic destinations, now run most of the year round. And the hard-sell by the travel agents begins in earnest in January for the summer holiday bookings. Holidays take a sizeable chunk out of a family's annual income, but people tend to regard this as an extravagance they would hate to do without. It is becoming more usual for people to take more than one main holiday a year, and holidays abroad are now common-place.

So it might come as a surprise to hear that there are some children who have never seen the sea. They have never been to the seaside, never made sandcastles on a beach nor paddled at the water's edge. These children come from all walks of life. Some are abused, many are from poor families, all are deprived of this natural childhood pleasure.

Nicky and Joanna are just two children who have never been on a holiday. In fact, they have had little enough to smile about since their father left home. Their mother longs to give them a treat, but it's all she can do to keep a roof over their heads. It is children like Nicky and Joanna that the Salvation Army helps by running summer camps on the coast where children can enjoy a fun-packed holiday.

Let me tell you how they helped Katy:

At just 11 years old, Katy was looking after her younger brothers and sisters because her father had deserted the family – and her mother, unable to cope, had turned to drink. The holiday the Salvation Army provided for Katy was her first and it transformed her from an unhappy young girl, burdened by responsibilities far beyond her age, into an excited child, splashing around in a swimming pool with her new friends, laughing and playing in the sunshine.

Here is part of a thank-you letter sent to the Salvation Army captain who organised a holiday:

Only a mother knows how it feels when her little boy sees the sea for the first time.

It did us both the world of good to get away. God bless you and the staff who gave us such a wonderful time.

Success stories such as these are happening all around the country, as a result of the Salvation Army's summer camps. And it isn't only children who benefit, as many lonely and elderly people too, are given a welcome break at these special centres.

Prayer

As we look forward to our own holidays, may we spare a thought for those people, children and adults, who for one reason or another will not be going away this year. If you know of someone in this situation, what could you do to let them know that you care?

Amen

3 Addiction

A new reader should take the middle section which speaks of Stella.

When William Booth began the Salvation Army in Victorian London, there was much squalor and misery. One means of escape for poor people was through the pleasures of drinking. But William Booth and his followers saw the dreadful results of drunkenness: the way it degraded people and led to violence in the home against wives and little children. For this reason, the Salvation Army has always preached abstinence from social drugs; and its uniformed members have to take a pledge not to drink any alcohol nor to smoke.

Today, living conditions are better for most of us than they were in Victorian England, yet people still turn to drink, cigarettes and other forms of drugs for comfort and to escape from their problems. When Salvationists come across such people, they do not judge them or sermonise about it, but they offer practical help. The Salvation Army runs rehabilitation centres where addicts can be helped to come off drugs and helped to cope with life without them.

Not all drug addicts are teenagers looking for a 'fix', or drunken old men. This is the story of an attractive woman who fell victim to drugs;

When The Salvation Army Captain first saw Stella, she was in a terrible state. Left by her husband three years earlier, for a younger woman, she was overwhelmed with depression.

She lived like a recluse, and was totally dependent on tranquillisers. Confused and shut away from the outside world, the more unhappy she felt, the more drugs she took.

It took five months of The Salvation Army's help for Stella to break free of her habit. Now she takes a keen and active part in life – and helps out at her local Salvation Army centre, to which she owes so much.
(The Caring Touch)

Prayer

Drugs may be attractive: they may help us to feel socially acceptable, they may be exciting, they may offer an escape from all the pressures that we feel. But drug *addiction* is not attractive. It robs us of our independence and leads to degrading behaviour.

We pray for all those who have fallen victim to drugs; and ask that we may have the strength of mind to withstand the temptations of drugs, and not to mock those who have decided to abstain completely from smoking and alcohol.

Amen

4   Lost and found

This is best read by adults or senior pupils, since the vocabulary is quite complicated. There are two clear sections.

When a loved one is reported missing, The Salvation Army Tracing Service swings into action. For decades The Salvation Army has been renowned for its high success rate in tracing missing persons both here and abroad, even helping police with their enquiries when all other avenues seem closed. As its director, Major Fairclough explains, the service exists primarily to trace 'known relatives in order to restore family relationships. In all cases, the best possible efforts are made to bring about a happy ending'.

There are many stories with happy endings. For example, after the First World War a British serviceman who wanted to be rid of his Armenian wife, managed to get her put into a mental institution in 1927. In 1990 a student social worker chatted with the old lady, still in care, and discovered that she had a daughter born in the early 1920s. Would it be possible to trace her? . . . Six months later her daughter was located and a joyful reunion took place. After 63 years of institutional life, Mrs G., now well into her 90s, lives happily in sheltered accommodation within walking distance of her daughter.

Amazing coincidences sometimes occur. One day an Aberdeen solicitor wrote to the Salvation Army on behalf of a client and his sister. They were seeking their brother, the 'black sheep' of the family, last seen at his mother's funeral. He was known to sleep rough under hedges or in Salvation Army hostels. That very day a letter also arrived from the rector of St. Martin-in-the-Fields Church, about a homeless man at his London centre wanting to trace his Scottish family whom he hadn't seen since his mother's funeral 17 years before . . .
(From a copy of 'Despatches')

The Salvation Army is a Christian Church which tries to put into practice the teachings of Jesus. Jesus told several parables about being lost and found, the most famous of which is the story of the Prodigal Son. In this story the 'prodigal' or wasteful son persuades his father to let him have his inheritance. He promptly leaves home and squanders his money on wine, women and song. It is only when he is down and out, and his so-called friends have deserted him, that he comes to his senses and realises how well-off he had been at home. He returns home with his tail between his legs, ready to apologise to his father and ask to be taken on as a servant. But while he is still some way off, his father sees him and runs to greet him, rejoicing to have his son home again.

Jesus told this parable to teach people about God. God is like the father in the story, giving people free will to make their own decisions about how they use their lives, but always willing to forgive mistakes and give people another chance. God rejoices when the lost are found.

Prayer

There will be times in our lives when we will feel lost: we will make mistakes and not know where to turn. Loving Father, may we know that you are there waiting for us, even when we have turned our backs on you.

Amen

MARIE CURIE CANCER CARE

1   Marie Curie

Display the caption: 'Care today – Cure tomorrow'

Marie Sklodowska was born in Poland in the nineteenth century. Her father was a school teacher in Warsaw so that, although her family was poor, Marie was well educated. As she grew up, she continued to be interested in science and went on studying in the evenings after work. She was so clever that she managed to get a job in the Faculty of Science at the University of Paris. In those days it was unusual for women to have such positions.

Marie was totally dedicated to her work and had little time for socialising. But she met another scientist, Pierre Curie, and they got married. It was expected that she would now give up work, but Marie was driven by a desire to help people through her work, and Pierre agreed that they should continue to work together.

In 1902 the couple made a great discovery. They were working with uranium which gives off radiation, and discovered that these rays came from a substance which they called radium. This discovery has been very important in medical science because radiotherapy – treatment with radiation – is now one of the main forms of cancer treatment. Pierre and Marie Curie were awarded the Nobel Prize for this discovery.

This is why the Marie Curie Memorial Foundation is named after Marie Curie. It is a charity concerned with cancer care. Most of us will have heard of someone, or know someone, who has cancer. Nearly one in three people have some form of it in their lifetime. Because so many of us have been personally touched by cancer, we want to do something about it. But the dilemma is whether to support a charity which researches into cures for cancer, or one which gives comfort and support to those who already suffer from it. Marie Curie does both, as its motto 'Care today – Cure tomorrow' proclaims.

It is Britain's leading cancer care charity, providing 11 residential centres nationwide and 5,000 community nurses; together with a research institute and an education and training programme for health care professionals. In 1991 4,000 patients were cared for in its residential centres, and 17,000 in their homes. It is now extending its work by building a day-care unit at the Edinburgh Marie Curie Centre.

This charity believes that 'no one should have to cope with cancer alone. People with this illness need care, emotional and other support 24 hours a day'. The Marie Curie Community Nurses fulfil this vital need, providing specialist nursing care for cancer sufferers in their homes, as well as being counsellors, advisers and friends to the families involved. One letter of thanks to the organisation said this:

Without them I could not have managed. When I tell you the last words I could understand from him were 'best at home', you will know how grateful I must be . . .

Prayer

Lord, we give thanks for the dedication and skills of scientists working for the good of others in medical research, and of doctors and nurses working in our hospitals, general practices and with patients in their homes.

We pray that, like Marie Curie herself, we too will want to use our abilities for the good of others.

Amen

2 Something for nothing

A collection of suitable items could be used as visual aids e.g. individual children could hold up each of the starred items as they read them out. You may wish to start a school collection, and to add something about this before the prayer.

Blue Peter is famous for its annual appeals on behalf of a charity. This popular television programme manages to enthuse children across the country into collecting all sorts of things which can be given directly to a charity or, more often, sold for funds. Other charities, too, often make appeals for unwanted odds and ends which, on their own, are hardly worth anything, but when collected in quantity can raise a tidy sum. You may see charity collecting boxes at airports, for example, for you to give away any foreign coins you have over from your holiday.

Marie Curie Cancer Care has a special 'Marie Curie Collection'. It appeals for the following items to be sent to one of their Freepost addresses:

★ Petrol vouchers

★ Air mile coupons

★ Used or unused postage stamps

★ Foreign coins

★ Trading stamps

★ Tea cards

★ Medals and badges

★ Unusual buttons

★ Postcards – old or new, blank or written

This is a way of helping charities to raise money without it really costing us anything apart from a little thought and effort. How often do we just throw things away which might be valuable to someone else? Think of all the things we've got tucked away at home which we never use, but which a charity might find some use for?

Charity shops are now a regular feature of any high street. They too, help people to recycle their goods to the benefit of all.

Next time we have a good clear out, to make room for some new clothes or our latest acquisitions, let us remember that charities can usually make good use of the things we are discarding.

Prayer

There is a proverb: He who wastes not, wants not.

It is easy for us, in our society, to develop a disposable mentality: things are made for convenience and not necessarily to last; fashions change; we get fed up with things; it's nice to have something new.

May we be more caring about our possessions – whether we keep them for ourselves or pass them on for others to make use of.

Amen

3   Daffodils

Display the slogan 'Care today – Cure tomorrow'.
Have a large bunch of daffodils on display in a prominent position.
For dramatic effect, have the reader of Nurse Mackman's part in
uniform; and the reader of Joan's part in a wheel-chair (improvised if
necessary) and pretending to be writing the letter.

Daffodils – bright spring flowers – they cheer us up after the long, dark winter and turn our thoughts to sunny days ahead. They are symbols of hope for the future.

Daffodils are worn by Welsh people on St. David's Day, the 1 March, because they are one of the emblems of Wales and their Patron Saint. They are also worn on 21 March by supporters of Marie Curie Cancer Care. On this Daffodil Day, supporters take to the streets to hand out daffodils to raise funds for this charity. People are encouraged to wear their daffodils – either real flowers or lapel stickers – as a celebration of hope.

You may think it strange to connect hope with cancer. One of the Marie Curie nurses explains:

(Nurse Nancy Mackman)
For many years the daffodil has been used to represent our work because it is a symbol of hope. And that's a word I hear a lot in my job, because for many people with cancer, having hope is one of the things that keeps them going.

This was brought home to me only recently after talking to Joan, a patient I look after at the Marie Curie Care Centre where I work. Her determination not to give up hope moved me so much I have asked her to write down her thoughts so you can see for yourself what an inspiration she is to so many nurses and other cancer patients.

(Joan)
Dear Friends,
As a patient in a Marie Curie Care Centre I am glad to share my experience of the excellent nursing I am receiving here.

Although crippled and terminally ill with cancer, I find life incredibly sweet. The staff, from domestics to doctors, create an atmosphere that is spiritually uplifting, while their specialist knowledge of pain-control provides help on a physical level . . .

Here, cancer has become a disease to live with, not a terrifying illness with death as the only outcome . . .

Yours faithfully,
Joan

(Nurse Nancy Mackman)
After reading this letter I'm sure you'll agree that if sheer will-power and courage could cure cancer, Joan would be back on her feet in no time at all.

Yet it is because there is still a lot of mystery surrounding cancer that Marie Curie Cancer Care is so important to thousands of patients like Joan, helping them to keep their hope alive.

The vital work being carried out at our Marie Curie Research Institute, for instance, is contributing to scientific advances in cancer research. As new discoveries are made in the fight against cancer there is hope that one day soon we will find a cure.

Yet as Britain's leading cancer care charity, the care we give to cancer patients like Joan, *every day*, is the more important part of our work.
(From a letter to supporters from a Marie Curie nurse)

Prayer

We cannot live without hope.
Hope isn't just wishful thinking – 'If only things were different'.
Hope is deeply rooted in the human spirit –
the tendency to trust that good overcomes evil,
that life conquers death,
just as spring follows winter.
Life and death are mysteries,
but if someone dying of cancer can talk of being spiritually uplifted, and if a cancer charity can speak of 'Care today – and cure tomorrow', then surely we have grounds for hope.

Amen

IMPERIAL CANCER RESEARCH FUND

1   Fighting cancer

These paragraphs could be taken by different readers, with a female taking the part of Jackie in the last section before the prayer.

When people think of cancer research in this country, they probably think of the Imperial Cancer Research Fund. It is the largest independent cancer research institute in Europe, and is run almost entirely from donations. It funds more than 90 individual research groups, and works in close co-operation with other cancer research organisations both nationally and internationally. The money and effort put into cancer research in recent years is paying off. There have been big successes. The most common children's cancer is acute lymphoblastic leukaemia; but 75 per cent of patients now survive.

Another advance is in an improved way of treating certain brain tumours which is being pioneered at St. Bartholomew's Hospital in London. Radioisotopes are planted right in the centre of the tumour so that they kill the cancer cells without damaging the surrounding brain tissue. Forty seriously ill patients, including some children, have been treated since the project began. Most are now in remission (which means that the disease has been brought under control) and many have returned to leading normal lives. Zoe was one of the very first patients to receive an implant for the treatment of a brain tumour, and her mother Jackie was amazed at the speed of her recovery from the operation. She says,

Just one hour afterwards, Zoe was asking for a Wimpy and chips! Zoe had this operation in 1987 when she was 13. She was out of hospital after five days and back at school within a couple of weeks.

Now five years after treatment Zoe leads a normal life and only goes back to St. Bartholomew's for regular check ups. It seems like a miracle, because when Zoe was 17 months old it was found that she had a brain tumour, which was treated with radiotherapy. When this recurred, it was not possible for it to be treated in this way again, as she had already received the maximum exposure when she was a baby. Without the implant operation, it seemed as if there would have been no chance for Zoe.

(Most of this material is taken or adapted from the second edition of 'Conquest: News up-dates from the Imperial Cancer Research Fund')

Prayer

It is impossible for us to imagine the anguish that parents go through when they have a child with cancer; but we should be able to identify with a teenager who likes her Wimpy and chips. Cancer attacks one in every three of us at some time in our lives. We give thanks for the research which is making treatment kinder and more effective.

Amen

THE ELLENOR FOUNDATION

Hospice Care Team

1   An ordinary family

Up to five readers could present this, taking a paragraph each (two for the prayers).

Many of the charities we hear about are big, well-established organisations which may have celebrated their Golden Jubilees or even more than 50 years in existence. In contrast to these, The Ellenor Foundation is an infant, since it only began in 1985. Not only is it young, but it is also localised, working in the area of the Dartford and Gravesham Health Authority in Kent in the South East of England. It was started by an ordinary family like yours or mine. Yet it quickly became well known in the district and within five years, more than a thousand patients and their families had benefited from the very special help that this charity provides.

The Ellenor Foundation provides medical, nursing, spiritual and emotional care mainly for cancer patients, together with support for their families and friends. Many of us know someone who has died of cancer, and this charity was started by a family that went through this experience. First Norman, the father of the family, died of cancer after a long and painful illness, and four years later, their mother, Ellen died suddenly from a stroke. The Ellenor Foundation is named after both Ellen and Norman.

There were three grown up children. The eldest brother, Graham, was running a language school in Sweden when his father was taken ill, and he came back to England to help run his father's business. The daughter, Jan, was a Home Economics teacher at a local school; and there was another brother, Ian, who was a social worker. They had been able to nurse their father in the place he most wanted to be, in the familiar surroundings of his own home; and now they wanted to help others do the same. After careful research and preparation, and working closely with local doctors and hospitals, The Ellenor Foundation came into being. The speed with which it has grown and been taken to heart by the local community is evidence of the great need that it is meeting.

Prayer

Dear Lord, when we see things that need to be done, don't let us assume that only richer people or older people can do something about it. Please give us the courage, the confidence and the commitment to do all in our power to meet those needs.

Amen

As we are inspired by the example of this family, let us give thanks for any other families we know that are working for the good of others, perhaps by fostering children, or giving their free time to local youth organisations, or by rescuing a stray pet, or in any other way.

Amen

2   The hospice movement

A number of readers could take different paragraphs, with individuals reading the starred points.

By helping to care for the dying, The Ellenor Foundation is part of what is known as the Hospice Movement. In the Middle Ages a 'hospice' was a place run by monks or nuns to give food, shelter and medical care to travellers. Today, hospices are places where people are cared for who are seriously ill. The best known name behind the modern Hospice Movement is Dame Cicely Saunders, a doctor who has devoted her life to the care of the dying and who founded St. Christopher's Hospice in South London in 1967.

Here are some important principles of the Hospice Movement:

★ The last stage of a person's life is a very precious time, and people should be helped to make the most of it with their friends and family.

★ Patients who are dying should be made as comfortable and free from pain as possible, but without being drugged so heavily that they are unaware of what is happening. In this way they are helped to die with dignity.

★ There is a care and concern for the whole person (physical, mental and spiritual) and not just for the physical illness that they have. This means that patients are given time to talk about their concerns and their hopes. They are treated as people and not just as medical cases.

★ There is also care shown for the family and friends of the dying, which can continue long after their loved ones have died. When the strain of caring for someone who is dying has ended, the task of grieving has only just begun.

Teams of home nurses from St. Christopher's help patients to remain in their own homes as long as possible. Their carers probably need advice and reassurance and someone on the end of the telephone in case of emergencies. They also know that the hospice is there when it becomes too difficult for them to care for their loved ones at home any longer.

If you visit St. Christopher's Hospice you will find a bright, well-kept modern building with balconies looking out over attractive gardens. It is a cheerful, comfortable place, with lots of people around so that the patients can always find someone to talk with them. People are helped, as much as possible, to feel at home (some even have their pets to visit them).

The Ellenor Foundation was inspired by St. Christopher's which cared for Norman when he was dying of cancer. It provides care for the dying and their families through its nursing teams who work mainly in people's homes. It also has close links with the local hospitals, with one nurse who offers advice there in the specialised field of pain control. The Ellenor Hospice Care Team has specially trained doctors, nurses, a social worker, chaplain, medical secretary and someone who co-ordinates the work of nearly 50 volunteers. The voluntary workers may befriend families of the dying, drive them to hospital, take them out for pleasure or just spend time with the sick person for a few hours to relieve the carers. Volunteers also work in the Bereavement Care Team, helping to support people in their grief. Other volunteers are involved in fund-raising.

Prayer

We usually put death out of our thoughts – but what if we had only a little time to live? What would we most want to do before we died? . . .

We do not know how long we have to live, and every moment of our lives is precious. Help us, Lord, to make good use of the time that is given us.

Amen

3   Religious faith

Display the logo of a candle shining in the darkness (see p. 40).
Divide the paragraphs between different readers.

Graham is the Chairman of The Ellenor Foundation, which he and his younger brother and sister set up after the death of their parents. In a report on the first five years of this charity, he writes:

For me personally the past five years have been a tremendous privilege. I can remember back to the time when my father was first diagnosed with terminal cancer and felt that despite the pain and suffering God had allowed it to happen for a purpose. It was the experience of his illness and the care given by St. Christopher's Hospice that eventually led to the setting up of the Ellenor Foundation in 1985.
(Our First Five Years)

It is clear from this statement that Graham has a strong faith and trust in God. He and the rest of the family are committed Christians who prayed for God's guidance before setting up The Ellenor Foundation. All its paid workers are also Christians (from different denominations), and they meet regularly to pray for the people they are helping and for each other. The Foundation is established on Christian principles and seeks to promote the care and compassion that Jesus had for the dying and the bereaved.

The Ellenor Foundation's logo is a lighted candle shining out into the darkness because it sees its purpose as bringing

light into dark situations, hope where there is despair and warmth in the security of loving care.
(Our First Five Years)

The Ellenor Foundation will help people of all religions or of none, and its team will not take advantage of dying people to try to convert them to the Christian faith. But if asked directly about their own beliefs, they will, of course, answer honestly. Dying people often wonder about religious matters. So, those who work with the dying, especially for a religious organisation, must be prepared, for instance, to be asked whether they believe in life after death, or why God allows suffering.

When people are dying, they often have very deep thoughts. Time is too precious to waste on trivia. They look back over their lives and consider the good and the bad, the joys and the pains, the love and the rejections, the successes and the failures. They will try to make sense of it all. They may feel sorry for some things in the past and may want to try to put things right in the little time that is left to them. They may want to talk about their death, and their loved ones may find this very difficult and try to protect them from it. In fact, it is often the carers who have to be helped to face death more than the patients themselves.

Prayer

Looking back over our own lives, let us dwell for a moment on something good we have done . . . and on something we are sorry for . . . on something in our lives which has brought us happiness . . . and on something which has caused us pain. In looking at life as a whole, help us Lord to accept the give-and-take of life.

Amen

4   Interview with a nurse

*Two people are needed to present this: an interviewer (**I**) and Joy (**J**)
who doesn't wear a nurse's uniform. (P.S. Her name has been changed
for confidential reasons and also because she sees herself as part of a team
and therefore doesn't want to be named individually.)*

I: Joy is a Respite Care Nurse with The Ellenor Foundation. Here she
speaks about her work.

I: Joy, why did you apply to work for The Ellenor Foundation, after
working with the National Health Service for more than 30 years?
J: I have always been interested in hospice care, and wanted to work in a
Christian team that was concerned to care for the whole person.

I: What does your job entail?
J: I only work part-time: about two days a week, but the work is very
demanding emotionally. It is being with patients who are dying, and
giving their carers a break. Basically, I do whatever is needed. It may be
traditional nursing, or just listening and talking with the patients and the
people who are caring for them at home. It could even be driving a very
ill person to the coast to see the sea for the last time.

I: What qualities do you need for this work?
J: Map-reading skills! It can be quite difficult finding your way to an
unknown house on a dark night.
A sense of humour! You never know what to expect next when working in
people's homes.
Love of people and an ability to sympathise with their joys, griefs and
pain.
Sensitivity to their feelings.
And a love of animals! You mustn't mind the family pets. Last week was a
good example. On Tuesday I was met at the door by the largest dog I
have ever seen. While on the Thursday I came across the smallest dog,
jumping in and out of my patient's electric foot warmer. At another home
I had to be prepared to step over six cats which sat across the top of the
landing guarding my patient's room.

I: What is the most difficult part of your work?
J: Coping with the emotional side of it. It can be very draining.

I: So, how do you cope with that?

J: There is always another member of the team I can call on for help. Also, we discuss things together as a team and pray together. I couldn't manage without prayer.

I: What is the most rewarding part of your work?

J: Being privileged to see the courage with which some people face their illness and to be with couples who love each other so much. Also, being able to control the pain so that people can live the last days of their life with dignity.

I: Are you glad to be working for The Ellenor Foundation?

J: Yes. It's the most fulfilling job I've ever done. I am using all of my skills as a nurse, and also learning so much about life. It's also made me realise that my Christian faith is so relevant to life.

I: Thank you very much, Joy.

Prayer

Let us spend a few moments thinking about what we want to do with our lives. What would we find most satisfying? Are we called to serve others? To work with people in need in any way? . . . What qualities would we need to help others? . . . When things get tough, where would we turn for inner strength and external support? . . .

Amen

5   A hospice of hope for Romania

A number of readers will be needed for this.

The Ellenor Foundation was established by a family in South East
England to provide home-care for the dying and their families. It is well-
known in the Dartford and Gravesham area, and is an example of a local
charity which is meeting local needs.

But its latest venture is to care for people who are dying one-and-a-half
thousand miles away – in Romania.

Here in England, those receiving hospice care are usually adults, dying
from cancer. In Romania many of the dying are little children. Nothing
has touched the hearts of the British public more in recent years than the
plight of thousands of Romanian orphans abandoned by their parents to
hundreds of institutions throughout Romania. Some of these children
have fallen victim to the indiscriminate use of dirty syringes and have
been infected by the HIV virus. This has resulted in an appalling legacy
of suffering as more and more children develop full-blown AIDS.

Graham, the Chairman of The Ellenor Foundation, first visited Romania
in 1975 as a tourist, and a chance meeting with a family in Brasov led to a
lasting friendship and a deep interest in the country and its people. He
returned several times, both before and after the revolution and saw for
himself the havoc wreaked on the country by Ceausescu and his brutal
regime.

In the summer of 1990 the Ellenor Team received a visit from a
Romanian doctor who was looking after children with AIDS. It was
during this visit that Graham first began to think about the possibilities of
using the experience he had gained in founding The Ellenor Foundation
to help set up a hospice organisation in Brasov. A few months later he
returned to Romania and on the plane met Norman and Ann Daniels.
Norman is the leader of Poplars Church in Worksop. They discovered
that they shared a similar vision and decided to work together.

In January 1991 Ellenor launched its 'Romanian Appeal' to raise
£500,000 for the project. A Romanian cancer specialist was seconded by
the Brasov Health Authority to work with The Ellenor Foundation for
three months in England to study hospice care of the dying. He has now

returned to become the Medical Director for Casa Sperantei – the name of the new hospice, which means 'Home of Hope'. At this hospice, the dedicated medical staff will help control the pain and give loving care to the dying.

(Taken from 'Hospice "Casa Sperantei"', Issue no. 1, News '92)

Prayer

We give thanks for all those whose hearts have been touched to do something for the suffering people of Romania. From those of us who have given money, or collected food, clothing and toys; to those who have travelled to Romania with provisions and practical help; and those who have gone there to live and work at institutions like Casa Sperantei. We give thanks that there is within the human spirit a desire to respond to other people's suffering and the belief that we can bring hope to those in despair.

Amen

AMNESTY INTERNATIONAL

AMNESTY
INTERNATIONAL
BRITISH SECTION

1   How it began

Display the Amnesty International logo of a candle surrounded by barbed wire.
For dramatic effect, light an Amnesty International candle in a prominent position in the darkened hall/room as the first sentence is read. The first paragraph should be read 'off stage' so that the reader's light isn't seen. Switch on the lights at the beginning of the second paragraph.
Use different readers for the different paragraphs.
Use voices from the floor of the hall for the starred sentences.
N.B. If the readers find the words 'Amnesty International' a tongue twister, they could replace it with 'A.I.' after its first mention.

Just over 30 years ago, on Sunday 28 May 1961, a candle surrounded by barbed wire was lit in the church of St. Martin's-in-the-Fields, Trafalgar Square. It marked the beginning of a crusade by a British lawyer called Peter Benenson who called on people to work for the release of thousands of men and women imprisoned throughout the world for their political and religious beliefs. His appeal for the 'Forgotten Prisoners' appeared in the *Observer* newspaper and was copied in newspapers all over the world.

The response was immediate, and from a tiny office in Mitre Court, London, grew the world's largest international voluntary organisation dealing with human rights. Known as Amnesty International, it now has over a million members in more than 150 countries throughout the world. In 1977 it was awarded the Nobel Peace Prize for its 'activity for the defence of human worth against degrading treatment, violence and torture.' And the following year it won the United Nations Human Rights Prize.

Thousands of people are in prison because of their beliefs. Many are held without charge or trial. Torture and the death penalty are widespread. In many countries, men, women and children have 'disappeared' after being taken into official custody. Still others have been put to death without any pretence of legality: selected and killed by the governments and their agents.

These abuses – taking place in countries of widely different ideologies – demand an international response. The protection of human rights is a universal responsibility . . . This is the fundamental belief upon which the work of Amnesty International . . . is based.
(What Does Amnesty International Do?)

★ Amnesty International seeks the release of prisoners of conscience. That is, men, women and children detained anywhere in the world for their beliefs, colour, sex, ethnic origin, language or religion, provided they have neither used nor advocated violence.

★ Amnesty International opposes the death penalty, torture or other cruel, inhuman or degrading treatment or punishment of prisoners.

★ Amnesty International advocates fair and early trials for all political prisoners.

Amnesty International's work is based on principles set forth in the United Nations Universal Declaration of Human Rights . . .

These universal rights include:
    the right to freedom of expression, conscience and religion;
    to freedom from arbitrary arrest and detention;
    the right to a fair trial;
    the right to life, liberty and security of person;
    the right not to be tortured.
(What Does Amnesty International Do?)

Prayer

Close your eyes and picture a candle surrounded by barbed wire –
Amnesty International's logo.

What does barbed wire mean to you? Where is it used? How is it used to
protect property, to keep people out? Where is it used to keep people in?
What would happen to you if you tried to get through barbed wire?

Now think about the candle. It is burning brightly. Where do you see
candles? How do they make you feel? Why does Amnesty International
use this symbol of hope within the barbed wire?

Amen

2 Thirty years on

You could continue to display the Amnesty International logo.
You will need at least three readers: one to start the reading, one to read
the letter and one for the prayers.

In the last 30 years, more and more people have become aware of
Amnesty International: what it does and what it stands for. Journalists
regard Amnesty as the acknowledged source of reliable information on
matters concerning human rights. Even governments take note of
Amnesty's reports.

Amnesty's researchers read over a thousand newspapers and journals, as
well as government bulletins and transcriptions of broadcasts. Vital on-
the-spot information comes from the missions it sends overseas. And
sometimes news comes from less formal sources, like news of a prisoner
of conscience in Argentina whose name was passed on to Amnesty by an
English hitch-hiking couple who had heard about him.

If Amnesty's research indicates that a prisoner is in special danger and
needs immediate help, the call goes out within hours to its 50,000 strong
worldwide Urgent Action network. Each action can generate several
thousand appeals to the authorities in a matter of days. These campaigns
work because officials are sensitive to international criticism. One African
head of state complained that a deluge of letters arrives as soon as the
authorities detain someone for questioning.

The organisation is seen to be politically independent, criticising abuse of
human rights *wherever* it finds it, whether at home or abroad.

In a letter written in September 1991, the Director of Amnesty's British
Section explains more about its political influence:

Almost every week an Amnesty delegation visits the Foreign and
Commonwealth Office. It may be to brief an Ambassador or High
Commissioner about to go overseas. Or the visit might be with the United
Nations Department of the Foreign Office to discuss the UK's human rights
strategies.

When a minister goes abroad, or a Head of State visits this country, Amnesty
often provides briefings. This gives us the chance to raise our concerns and
bring pressure to bear at the highest levels of government. For example,

during his visit to China, the Foreign Secretary raised the cases of 20 Prisoners of Conscience.

Our information can have a direct influence on government decisions. Two days before the Minister for Overseas Development was due to visit Nigeria, she announced she was cancelling the trip because of the information we gave about executions there.

It's a tribute to Amnesty's reputation for accuracy that we have access to high level government officials. The Refugee Office sends to the Home Office a copy of our reports on the countries of origin of those seeking asylum in the UK . . . Amnesty continually lobbies the Home Office to introduce safeguards to prevent asylum seekers from being returned to countries where their lives or liberty could be at risk. We have had many successes in preventing people from being returned to face imprisonment, torture or death.

Over the last 30 years, Amnesty International has adopted or investigated more than 42,000 cases, involving one or more prisoners. For these Prisoners of Conscience, Amnesty may be their only hope for freedom and an end to their suffering.

Prayer

We pray for the numerous prisoners throughout the world who feel powerless in the hands of corrupt governments. Who are arrested, detained, often tortured and killed, without being given a fair trial.

We thank God that Amnesty International exists:
    to draw attention to those who are hidden away in prison cells;
    to speak for those who are forbidden to speak for themselves;
    to bring hope to the fearful;
    and to champion the rights of the helpless.

Amen

3 Write a letter

You could continue to display the Amnesty International logo.
For dramatic effect, have a different face painted on five large posters
with the starred words written on the back so that five readers read out
the information as each holds up his/her picture in turn.
The posters should continue to be held up while the next passage is read.
The readers of the letters could sit down at a table and pretend to be
writing them as they read them out.
N.B. If the readers find the words 'Amnesty International' a tongue-
twister, they could replace it with 'A.I.' after its first mention.

★ Morocco. – Mohamed Srifi. – Sentenced to 30 years for his peaceful political views. – Write to: His Majesty King Hassan II.

★ Malawi. – Vera Chirwa. – Jailed for believing that her country should be run differently. – Write to: His Excellency The Life President.

★ Philippines. – Maria Nonna Santa Clara. – 'Disappeared' with a colleague while working for a community organisation. – Write to: President Corazon Aquino.

★ China. – Wang Xizhe. – Jailed since 1981 for advocating democracy. – Write to: President Yang Shangkun.

★ Israel. – 'Abd Al-Ru'uf Ghabin. – Reported being tortured. – Please write to: Yitzak Shamir, Prime Minister of Israel.

('Amnesty' June/July 1991)

The detention of any prisoner of conscience violates the Universal Declaration of Human Rights. Amnesty International works for the immediate and unconditional release of *all* prisoners of conscience.

When the facts show that individuals are prisoners of conscience, the cases are usually allocated to one or more of the movement's groups around the world. The groups – comprising local Amnesty International members – study the background to the cases and then begin writing to the responsible authorities, appealing for the prisoners' immediate and unconditional release.

Letter after letter goes to cabinet ministers and prison officials. The members try to get publicity in the local press about the prisoner they are working to free. They go to the foreign embassy or trade delegation in their country.

They get prominent people to sign appeals. If they can contact the prisoner's family, they may send relief parcels and correspond with the prisoner.

For every prisoner of conscience whose case becomes news, there are many more who are unknown; and even those who gain wide publicity tend to be forgotten over time. Amnesty International aims to give attention to all forgotten prisoners, to ensure that they remain a public concern and that they are cared for individually, while the efforts to free them are underway.
(What Does Amnesty International Do?)

When confronted by horrific violations of human rights, you might think it strange that people just write letters – but it works! This is an extract from the Amnesty International letter-writing guide on the need for letters:

. . . you are part of a worldwide campaign in which thousands of others join. This steady stream of letters from all corners of the globe can and does have an effect on governments. Our files contain many letters from prisoners who have told us they believe they were released or spared from torture or execution as a result of this type of international pressure.

In May 1984, 18 year old Florence Nnakandi was arrested by Ugandan soldiers and taken to a barracks where she was repeatedly assaulted and tortured. She was not charged with any offence. Amnesty International launched an Urgent Action appeal. In September two further appeals were made when it was learned that she was still being held without charge – with her critically ill baby daughter, aged eight months.

Dear Sir,
I am a student from an English school and a member of Amnesty International. I have been greatly disturbed to hear of the arrest of Florence Nnakandi and that she has been imprisoned for months now without being charged. I write to appeal to you on humanitarian grounds to release her immediately.
Yours sincerely . . .

Thanks to such pressure, this young woman is now free. This is what she wrote after her release:

Dear Friends,
I write to thank you from the bottom of my heart for everything you did for me and my baby when we were in custody.

You wrote letters to the Uganda authorities protesting against my arbitrary arrest and detention without trial. I know of these letters through the Leader of the Opposition. These letters were a great consolation to me. I believe these letters influenced the Government when they decided to release me.

I am now reunited with my dear mother, my brothers and sisters and my friends.
I thank you most sincerely.
Florence Nnakandi.

Prayer

How often have we seen something wrong – something we object to – and yet we are too frightened or too apathetic or too busy to do anything about it? Or we complain loudly but are not prepared ourselves to alter the situation.

Help us, Lord, to be active in defence of what we care about. Give us the courage and the wisdom to deal with situations tactfully but firmly. Help us to defend those who, for whatever reason, cannot defend themselves.

Amen

4   Education for freedom

You could continue to display the Amnesty International logo.
For dramatic effect, the second paragraph could be read out slowly with
pupils miming the different money-raising efforts described there.
It would make most sense of the material if the first half were read by
pupils and the second half by teachers.

Norway – 25 October 1990 – tens of thousands of boys and girls obey the call of their unions – and walk out of school! A protest? A strike? No – this was 'Operasjon Dagsverk' – Operation A Day's Work, their annual event to raise money for charity to help young people overseas to defend their own rights and those of others.

The students work cleaning floors, washing cars, chopping wood, gardening, working in farms, offices, garages and factories. If they can't find paid work they go out on the streets, cleaning shoes, selling coffee, juggling, busking, dancing, singing, begging, shaking cans.

In 1990 they picked Amnesty International as their charity and over £2 million was raised that day. The money went to a project called 'Teaching for Freedom'. This is to help developing sections of Amnesty International in Asia, Africa and Latin America in a six-year campaign to educate the youth of their countries about human rights.

The Norwegian Section of Amnesty International had organised an intensive campaign in every secondary school before the event with teach-ins, posters, leaflets, films and talks about the work of Amnesty around the world, and how human rights education could prevent human rights abuse. The participants knew exactly what they were working for.

(Adapted from 'Amnesty', February/March, 1992)

Here in this country too, Amnesty International is supporting schools in education about human rights. When the History document of the National Curriculum for England and Wales was being finalised, Amnesty International mounted a letter-writing campaign to MPs. In a leaflet entitled *Human Rights Education – A right for all?* the organisation made this appeal:

Amnesty International is asking individual members, particularly parents, teachers and school governors in England and Wales to write a letter immediately to their MP to press for the inclusion of human rights education in the National Curriculum, and in particular teaching about the United Nations and the Universal Declaration of Human Rights.

The purpose of teaching about human rights is to give young people the knowledge, understanding and skills to meet the challenges and responsibilities of citizenship in the modern world. Freedom, equality and justice are concepts essential for the understanding of democracy and of basic rights such as the right to life and liberty proclaimed in the Universal Declaration of Human Rights.

Now that it has been included as a compulsory part of the National Curriculum, Amnesty International is producing educational materials to support teachers in this task.

Prayer

In a democracy where we tend to take human rights for granted, help us Lord to value our freedoms, to be aware of abuses of human rights, both in our own country and abroad, and to champion the rights of others.

Amen

WATERAID

1   The water decade

Use different voices for the information on each year. These readers could come onto the stage one by one with a poster showing their year.

The United Nations called the 1980s the Water Decade. They wanted us, in these ten years, to help people in parts of the world where they suffered from lack of water and from contaminated water supplies.

1981
WaterAid was founded as the British Water industries' response to the Water Decade.

1982
The first self-help project was funded. WaterAid provided £210 for cement and transport for three wells in Zambia. These provided 300 people with safe water.

1983
WaterAid's first Resident Engineer took up his post in Sierra Leone.

1984
The first WaterAid appeal was sent out with water rates bills by North Surrey Water Company.

1985
The Country Programmes for Uganda, Tanzania and India began.

1986
The Gambia and Nepal Country Programmes began.

1987
WaterAid's annual income exceeded £1 million for the first time.

1988
Over 20,000 water industry employees and pensioners gave regularly to WaterAid through lotteries and payroll giving.

1989
WaterAid's annual income exceeded £2 million.

1990

The total funds raised by WaterAid since 1981 exceeded £10 million.

1990 was the last year of the UN Water Decade, but WaterAid continues to improve the lives of millions of people by assisting local organisations in developing countries to continue and extend the work which they have begun. The WaterAid Journal for Spring 1991 considers the main reason for its success:

From the outset, the distinctive thing about WaterAid has been its relationship with the British water industry. Of course many other industries have their associated charities. But normally these are concerned with the welfare of the industry's employees or pensioners, or with the needs of communities in which the industry is sited. The British water industry is unique in sponsoring a charity concerned to address the same human needs which it itself addresses, but to do so in parts of the world where those needs are particularly acute.

The industry and its employees have been at the root of WaterAid's growth through staff lotteries, appeals to consumers, donations from the newly privatised companies and many other initiatives . . . As a result WaterAid now has a recurrent income of almost £3 million a year. Only about 100 of almost 200,000 registered charities in Britain are larger than that.
(*'Oasis', the WaterAid Journal, Spring 1991*)

Prayer

There is a saying: 'Charity begins at home' – and some people use this as a reason for not giving to charities which help people overseas. It is particularly impressive, then, that the British water industry and those who work for it have made a commitment to improve the water supplies of people in countries far away.

We give thanks for people's generosity and for the human capacity to show love even for those who are beyond our nearest and dearest.

Amen

2   The first steps to health

There are clear sections here for a number of readers. With a little imagination, the first paragraph could be illustrated through simple drama to catch the listeners' attention.

Everyone needs water. We cannot live for more than a few days without it. In fact, we are mostly water – 2/3 of our body weight and 9/10 of our body volume is water. Water seems plentiful, covering about three quarters of the earth's surface, but most of it is salt water in oceans or frozen water in polar regions. The fresh water needed by humans is less than 1 per cent of the world's supply, and even that is unequally distributed. In the rich countries, people use on average 190 litres of water per person per day, compared to about 35 litres per person per day in an African village.

In hot climates, people need a great deal of drinking water just to stay alive. Not surprisingly, people are more concerned with the quantity of water they are drinking than the quality, but quality is of utmost importance. In the developing world, children suffer because they do not have a clean, safe water supply. The majority of these children do not live in drought stricken countries, but for many of them the local water supply is the unknown deadly enemy – the carrier of diseases such as diarrhoea, typhoid and dysentry – which each year kill over 3 million young children.
(*UNICEF UK, Information Sheet No. 9*)

From 1983 to 1985 Timothy Goodacre worked as a surgeon at Mvumi Hospital in central Tanzania. The following descriptions are taken from notes he made during his time there, parts of which have been published in the WaterAid journal.

When I was working at Mvumi the whole water and sanitation system had fallen into disrepair. Our own house was on the lowest part of the site and normally had some sort of water supply (except when the borehole pump broke down), but the operating theatre was at a high level and scrubbing-up before an operation merely meant a nurse pouring jugs of water from a bucket over my hands. There was rarely any water in the adjacent surgical wards. An overground sewage pipe regularly sprayed its contents onto unwary passers by. Foul effluent from broken-down toilets had to be pushed across a corridor between two wards to reach the only working drain. The old sewage disposal pits were close to the hospital buildings and a potent source of malaria: I well recall, when out on my early morning jog, taking a huge gulp of breath before reaching them and trying to hold it until I'd passed the dreadful pong. . . .

On returning to Mvumi again in November 1987 . . . the situation on the wards had improved beyond belief: each had running water, a sink, and the toilets worked. There was a constant supply to the operating theatre scrub tank, and even a toilet there too . . . The work is a credit to WaterAid's Engineer and his team of local Tanzanians, who are now taking over the maintenance. Mvumi now has appropriate and well designed water and sewage installations which should carry it into the next century. Without them a hospital which has served an enormous population in Tanzania for many years must have slowly crumbled away for want of basic services.
(*'Oasis', the WaterAid Journal, Autumn 1988*)

Prayer

Let us give thanks for the gift of water:
clean, fresh water to quench our thirst;
a bath full of hot water to relax in,
or a shower to refresh us;
plenty of water to wash and rinse our clothes;
water to keep things clean;
water for the garden;
water for life.

Amen

3   H$_2$O

You will need a big poster for the slogan, with H$_2$O standing out clearly on it. The readings fall easily into sections for four readers.

What is the scientific formula for water?   H$_2$O

When you next use that formula, I want you to remember this slogan from WaterAid:

Help Others

2

help themselves

In its various projects to improve the water supplies in developing countries, WaterAid has provided technical advice and funding for the materials, but it has always encouraged people in the developing countries to do as much as possible for themselves, as this article explains:

People in Britain think of water supply and sewerage as services which are provided for them by specialist companies; they expect to play no part in creating those services themselves. In the world's poorest countries, where hundreds of millions of people lack water and sanitation, WaterAid knew that that would not be realistic.

To keep down costs, and to create a sense of local ownership and caring, ordinary people needed to be involved in planning and building simple, practical and low-cost improvements: whether by digging wells, protecting springs, laying pipes, building latrines or whatever.

WaterAid's policy has, therefore, always been to support projects not just *for* the poor, but which would be constructed mainly *by* the poor themselves. Enthusiasts within and beyond the British water industry immediately welcomed this self-help ethic, and found it something which they very much wanted to support.

So, what WaterAid has demonstrated first and foremost in the last 10 years is the willingness and ability of some of the poorest people in the world to make real improvements to their own water supplies and sanitation.

(*'Oasis', the WaterAid Journal, Spring 1991*)

This example comes from a BBC radio producer:

I had been in East Africa for a few days only, before I realised that in a country as desperate as Uganda some forms of aid work, and others don't.

A simple 'hand-out' approach – except in the case of immediate crisis care – doesn't work. People receiving that sort of aid inevitably come to rely on it, and therefore become increasingly dependent on the ebb and flow of money from the developed countries of the world.

That's why I was particularly impressed by the work of WaterAid. A clear commitment to operate only with the full co-operation of the local community must be the best way forward. I saw it paying off in several remarkable ways.

We went to a village not far from Lake Victoria where water was about to be connected to standpipes and would benefit 4,000 people. Everyone was thrilled at the prospect of safe water for all. No longer would the women and children of the village have to walk down a steep hill to a dirty stream, and carry infected water back uphill to their homes. And they'd done most of the trench-digging and building themselves. They had an understandable pride in what they had achieved with help from their friends in WaterAid. As soon as the WaterAid Land Rover bounced its way into the centre of the village we were surrounded by dozens of adults and countless children, all eager to show their appreciation for the work of Ruth Deer, the country co-ordinator, and her staff.

(*'Oasis' the WaterAid Journal, Winter 1989*)

Prayer

Many people hate to be dependent on charity or to ask someone for help. We all have our pride and self-respect, and it makes us feel good when we can achieve something on our own. WaterAid realised this when working in developing countries, but we should also be aware of this when helping friends and people around us – whether we are giving a hand with someone's homework, or teaching them to use a piece of equipment like a computer or a keyboard.

Lord, don't let us help people in order to make *ourselves* feel good; but give us the patience to encourage and help people to help themselves – in order that *they* might feel good.

Amen

SIGHT SAVERS

1   Some causes and cures of blindness

Use a variety of readers, and a different one for each of the starred sections.

Which of your five senses is most precious to you? If you had to do without one of your senses, which would you choose: the sense of smell – taste – touch – hearing – or sight? Of course, all five senses are important and we depend on them all, but many people would say that the most precious of all is our eyesight. How would we manage without it? Those of us who wear glasses or contact lenses know what it is like to see things out of focus; and if you have ever been blindfolded, you know how helpless and vulnerable you feel. We can all begin to imagine what blindness must be like. Try opening your eyes in a pitch-black room and you'll have the strange sensation of looking but not being able to see anything.

Do you know the main cause of blindness? . . .

It is POVERTY! In Great Britain there are about three thousand blind children. In Africa three *hundred* thousand. Ninety per cent of blind and partially sighted children live in the developing countries. And what is so tragic is that most of these blind children were born with normal eyesight, but lost their sight during the first few years of life.

What causes most of these children to go blind?

★ Children can go blind from lack of vitamin A, which we get from dark green leafy vegetables like spinach, and from red and yellow fruits and vegetables like carrots. The common childhood disease of measles can drain a child's reserves of vitamin A and leave the child blind. In this country children are immunised against measles, and those who catch it are protected from its worst effects by good diets and medicines.

★ Trachoma is another cause of blindness in developing countries where there are overcrowded and unhygienic conditions, and where there is a lack of clean water to wash hands and face. Repeated infection turns

66

the eye-lashes in upon the eyeball until every blink is agony as it scratches the eye. Without treatment a sufferer will eventually go blind.

★ Another cause of blindness is cataract, which is a milky clouding over of the eyes. This usually happens to people as they grow old, but it can also affect children. It is estimated that there are between 17 and 20 million people in the world who are blind from cataract. Yet it is curable. All it needs is a simple operation to remove the opaque lens from the eye. Within three days the patient can return home, wearing glasses, with sight restored. The operation takes about 15 minutes and costs as little as £8.

Sight Savers is the name of a charity which raises money to prevent and cure blindness. It started in 1950 as the Royal Commonwealth Society for the Blind. Since 1987 it has been called Sight Savers and its work now extends beyond the Commonwealth countries. By 1991, working with its partners overseas, Sight Savers had provided 3 million eye operations to restore sight, and treated 30 million more people to prevent blindness.

Sight Savers brings eye care services to the world's poorest people. It knows that in 70 per cent of cases blindness can be prevented. It trains health workers to recognise early signs of eye problems: to provide treatment and to teach mothers the importance of providing vitamin A for their children from cheap, available fruit and vegetables. It also provides eye hospitals and mobile eye units.

Prayer

In a few moments of silence let us give thanks for all of our senses, and particularly for the use of our eyesight . . . We think especially of any blind people known to us personally, and pray that all blind people will be given the courage to cope with their disability . . . We pray for all those who help blind people: medical workers and those involved in charities like Sight Savers, those who run these charities and those who support them . . . May we all work for a world in which the 70 per cent preventable blindness will be prevented and the millions of poor people with cataracts will be provided with the facilities for sight-saving operations.

Amen

2   Turn the tide on blindness

Display the slogan 'Turn the tide on blindness'.
Use a variety of readers.

A slogan of Sight Savers is 'Turn the tide on blindness'. This is the slogan for their campaign to prevent river-blindness in African countries. It is estimated that river-blindness has claimed 600,000 victims worldwide, but it is found particularly in West Africa and parts of central Africa. In the 1950s, when Sight Saver's founding director visited northern Ghana he spoke of 'The country of the blind'.

River blindness is caused by parasitic worms which are spread by the bite of the black simulium fly. The fly carries the larvae of tiny worms which breed in a victim's skin, causing inflammation and itching. The worms' offspring can eventually invade the eye and lead to several years of suffering before causing blindness. These flies breed around the rivers where people often work.

In badly affected areas nearly half of the adult men may be blind. This has serious social consequences, as Djiba's story illustrates.

Djiba Konate from Guinea was only 39 when his sight began to deteriorate; now, ten years later, he is blind. During that time his family has changed from being self-sufficient to depending on charity.

When Djiba could work at full capacity the family field produced enough food for nine months of the year, and he used to migrate to neighbouring Ivory Coast during the dry season to earn money to see them through the rest of the year.

For the past four years the household has endured severe food shortage, often eating only one meal a day, which might be just manioc leaves mixed with salt and oil. Recently Djiba's two young sons, 15-year-old Mory and Bandjan who is only 11, have been trying to cultivate the plot. Both boys are very undernourished and miss a lot of time through illness; when they do go to the field, hunger and fatigue limit the amount of work they can do.

Their mother Tenen devotes all her energies to meeting the daily food needs and running the household – which also includes a daughter who went blind. Tenen makes a little money by selling fish, but at times of desperate shortage she goes back to the village where she was born to beg for food. Neighbours

68

help too, but Djiba sees no hope of an improvement in his family's situation. (*'Horizons', Autumn 1991*)

Sadly, it is too late for those who have already gone blind through this disease, but there *is* hope for others in these infected areas. The progress of the disease can be halted by a simple pill called ivermectin, which needs to be taken only once a year. These pills have been donated free by the manufacturers, but it is a costly business to publicise their use in village communities and to organise and record their distribution. It is estimated that it costs £1 a year for each patient.

Science has provided the cure, but it is people's kindness, through organisations like Sight Savers, which can now make this medicine available to poor people who cannot afford it. Science is a tool for us to use, but *how* we use it is a matter of our values: of what we believe is right and what we are prepared to do about it.

Prayer

Dear Lord, help us to use science in the service of humanity.

Science can provide answers; but first we have to ask the right questions.
Science is knowledge; but what we do with that knowledge depends on our priorities.
Science is a means to an end; but not the end in itself.

What questions should we be asking to improve life on earth?
What should our priorities be?
And what ends are we seeking?

Lord, help us to seek the good of all humanity,
and to do all in our power to see that science is put to good use.

Amen

OXFAM

1   Still time

You will need a tape-measure 30 cm long, with the first 12 cm coloured red (you can make one from paper). It could be demonstrated on a pupil. A number of readers may be used.

Take a look at this tape-measure. The first 12 cm are coloured red. Oxfam teams in developing countries use tapes like this one to measure starvation. Malnutrition can be quickly assessed by using this measuring tape around the middle of a young child's upper arm. The red zone shows severe malnutrition. For a child to have a measurement of 12 cm or less, it must have virtually no flesh on its upper arm. The fact that these tapes are used is tragic.

For 50 years Oxfam has helped countless men, women and children to escape from situations of terrible poverty – bringing hope to those in desperate need. Yet the gap between the rich and poor of this world continues to widen. During the 1980s average incomes in the UK rose by 20 per cent; in Africa and parts of Latin America they fell by between 10 and 25 per cent. In the rich countries 25 per cent of the world's population consume 80 per cent of the earth's resources. And a small child dies every two and a half seconds from poverty. The suffering goes on, despite the efforts of aid agencies like Oxfam, because wars stop the production of food and force people to leave their homes, because floods and droughts lay waste their land, because of the falling price of their cash crops on the world market . . . the reasons are varied and complex, but the result is always the same – suffering for the poor.

While this situation prevails, Oxfam will continue to challenge poverty in the Developing World and its causes. While it is always ready to help in disasters, it believes that the solution to poverty is long-term development which helps people to help themselves, rather than handouts. In its 50th anniversary year, instead of looking back on all its achievements in helping individuals rise above poverty – it set out resolutely on the next 50 years. It started its 50th anniversary on 1 October 1991 with a new campaign entitled 'It's time for a Fairer World'. It asked people to pledge their *time* to help Oxfam, or to send £25 to buy a day's time. It was apt that 1992 was a leap year when we have an extra day the 29 February. Oxfam appealed for people to give *them* that extra day's work or its equivalent in money. It was aiming at one million days by Oxfam's 50th birthday in October 1992.

Prayer

Sometimes, time is not very important to us – in the long summer holidays, for instance, when we may have 'time on our hands'. At other times, every minute is precious – in an exam, for example. People at work realise that time is precious, and may say 'time is money' – many are paid by the hour. Voluntary work takes time. It may be just as hard as paid work, and just as valuable, but it is unpaid.

How do we use our time? . . . How much spare time do we have? . . . Do we spend enough of it in freely helping others? . . . We pray that we will be responsible with this valuable resource that each of us has been given.

Amen

2 Disasters

You may wish to use this with news of a current disaster – thinking of the needs of disaster victims in a particular situation.
Use a number of readers, particularly for the starred points.

When a disaster strikes anywhere in the world, we soon hear about it on the radio and see pictures of the devastation on our television screens. Certain parts of our planet are susceptible to earthquakes, volcanoes, tidal waves, hurricanes, droughts and other natural disasters. Those who suffer most are almost always the poor. People who have barely enough to get by at the best of times, cannot afford to protect themselves against natural disasters. In such emergencies, there are five major charities which always respond and to which the public can send their donations: they are Oxfam, Save the Children Fund, Christian Aid, CAFOD (the Catholic Fund for Overseas Development), and the Red Cross or Crescent.

What sort of help is needed in such disasters?

On 30 April 1991 a cyclone struck coastal districts of Bangladesh. Within hours, it had killed a hundred and fifty thousand people and left four million homeless. Bangladesh, one of the poorest countries in the world, appealed for international aid to help the survivors who were facing starvation and disease. Their animals, crops and food supplies had been washed away. Their land and homes were still knee-deep in water. Drinking water supplies were contaminated. And all this came on top of the shock and sorrow of bereavement. Along with the other charities, Oxfam, was able to respond promptly. Within the week, it had spent nearly £170,000 on food supplies; as well as mobilising a medical team and volunteer water engineers to sink 30 wells for clean drinking water.

Oxfam has a special Disasters Appeal so that it is able to respond quickly at times such as this. In asking for donations, it tells us that £23 will buy five blankets for people like these flood victims, and £42 will buy enough tablets to purify 10,000 litres of water. Oxfam's Disasters Appeal wants to ensure the following:

★ To make sure their emergency stores are full, because they never know when the next call for help will come.

★ To have emergency and technical teams trained to respond.

★ To be able to employ local people to organise the relief, who are already on the scene with a good knowledge of the situation.

★ Once the disaster has passed, Oxfam wants to help people rebuild their lives.

★ Oxfam also wants to stop future disasters from occurring, where these can be foreseen and prevented.

Prayer

Dear Lord, we feel so small and helpless in the face of major natural disasters. They can seem so remote, when they are happening in some distant part of the world. But our gift, however small, can help – to buy purifying tablets for polluted drinking water, or a blanket to keep someone warm who has lost their home. May we never become immune to news of disasters and human misery.

Amen

3   Women's work

Use a number of readers, preferably female.

A photograph in *Oxfam News* shows people harvesting crops. The slogan reads: 'These farmers work 12 hours a day in the tropical heat . . . then they go home to cook dinner.' It goes on to tell us that many of the world's farmers are women. They grow half the world's food. Most also have to look after children, keep house, and collect water and firewood. It is quite usual for women in developing countries to work 16 hours a day. Yet in the past these women were seldom consulted when aid projects were set up in their villages. In recent years, development agencies have been becoming more aware that it is essential to consult with women and for women to participate in decisions affecting their lives.

In Ethiopia, an Oxfam-funded water pump programme did not work because the women who collected the water had not been consulted about their needs. The pumps were difficult to maintain, and the round bottomed containers they used for water wouldn't stand up on the concrete walls around the wells. Pumps have since been abandoned in favour of open wells, and stands have been provided for the containers. Oxfam now tries to ensure that women are consulted so that they benefit from all its projects.

Tisuake Zulu, a mother of six, reflects on the difference made to her life by one such project. Tisuake, like most other women of Zambia, feeds, cares for and brings up her children in the face of rising malnutrition and widespread poverty. Her husband hovers on the edge of her life. He has three other wives, and does not support Tisuake's children. As a woman, Tisuake does not have the right to divorce him, nor is she allowed credit. Such rules governing women's lives vary from culture to culture, but are common to most communities in developing countries. They conspire to keep women poor and powerless, with little control over decisions that affect them. This, despite the fact that economies depend on them. Women do two-thirds of the world's work.

Tisuake joined together with 15 other women in an agricultural project supported by Oxfam. They worked their plots of land together, sharing each other's burdens and the results of the work. As a group, they were able to get credit. At first they were growing cash-crops which needed

74

expensive fertilisers, but now they grow a variety of crops for cash and food. 'The results have been outstanding,' says Tisuake. 'This year I have no hunger in my house.' The project has renewed her confidence. The women have a say in their own affairs, and have begun to challenge traditional assumptions about the roles of men and women in the village.

(Adapted from 'Oxfam News', Spring 1992)

Prayer

We give thanks for all who have fought for the rights of women in this country, so that women can vote with men, have equal rights by law, and have considerable control over their own lives.

We pray for women who are oppressed and exploited – thinking especially of those in developing countries whose lives are very hard.

We celebrate the special qualities that women bring to family life and to the workplace.

Amen

CHRISTIAN AID

Christian Aid

1   Christian principles

Try to get a Christian Aid envelope and a Christian Aid Week poster as visual aids. You could draw attention to this year's slogan as well as the one mentioned in the passage below.
Pupils could mime the different responses to the Christian Aid collector.

The third week of May each year is Christian Aid Week, when churches throughout Britain organise door-to-door collections. The collectors have come to expect a variety of responses as they stand waiting on people's doorsteps.

★ Some people have the envelope ready and thank the collectors for their efforts.

★ Others talk about charity beginning at home.

★ Some give generously.

★ Others get rid of their small change.

★ Some give cheerfully.

★ Others bemoan the fact that so many people come knocking for money these days.

Many charities now have a designated week each year in which they are allowed to collect door-to-door. Christian Aid was the first charity to start this, and its supporters feel that all the effort they put into it is worthwhile. In 1991, for instance, a record £10 million was collected.

Most people have heard of Christian Aid because it has been around for so long, but although the name is familiar we may not actually know too much about it. Christian Aid started in Britain after the Second World War. It was a response of the Churches to the human tragedy of the refugees throughout Europe, made homeless by the war, often without families and bereft of the basic necessities of life. Christians of different Churches worked together to help provide for these people. They saw it as the Christian thing to do – in other words, what Jesus would have done if he were here.

As time went on, this crisis passed, but cries for help were now being heard from farther afield, beyond Europe. Television was bringing home to Christians in Britain the desperate needs of people in the Developing World, many of whom were struggling simply to stay alive. They remembered the story Jesus told about the Good Samaritan and his teaching on that occasion that our neighbour is anyone in need – and so Christian Aid became good neighbours to the needy throughout the world – whoever they were, of whatever creed or religion. It works where the need is greatest in more than 70 countries and is the official relief and development agency of many of the British and Irish Churches. In 1991 a slogan was coined for Christian Aid Week which read: 'We believe in life *before* death'. The Church believes in life *after* death, but it also believes in caring for people in this life and helping them to lead full and worthwhile lives here and now.

Prayer

How do we react when people come knocking on our door for charity? Do we think of thanking them for their trouble? Do we take an interest in what the charity is doing?

Do we believe that 'Charity begins at home'? If so, does it have to begin and end at home? Haven't we got neighbours throughout the world – fellow human beings whom we can help?

Amen

2   How it works

*You will need at least two readers, one of whom should be a female
dressed in a sari, pretending to write the letter as she reads it out.*

Christian Aid has its own Projects Officers for different areas of the
world, who form the link between the aid projects and Christian Aid
headquarters which funds them; but the projects themselves are run by
the people and organisations of the countries being helped. Christian Aid
does not send out relief workers as some other agencies do. It believes
firmly in giving responsibility for their development to the people
themselves.

In this letter from an Indian nun, we hear about a project that Christian
Aid supports in India, and also the common misunderstanding over
Christian Aid's name and purpose.

Dear Friends,

Greetings to you from Sister Celestine of Gollahalli! 'Gollahalli' as a name
may not mean anything to you. It is a remote Indian village where the
problems of poverty such as illiteracy, ill health, absence of clean water,
insufficient income and caste discrimination are our life.

Our organisation, SUNANDA, means 'Bringer of Joy'. It began here with the
help of Christian Aid in 1980. Starting work was not easy. We were
misunderstood as being there to make people Christians. But we were happy
when our slogan worked: 'We are not here to make you Christians. We are
here because we are Christians.' We were accepted.

Our involvement with the people has provided basic necessities such as
health and education. We encourage our people to participate in their own
development and work together to bring about change in their day to day
lives. We are aware that all their problems are not solved, but there are
milestones of hope in people like Pappamma who can now sign her name
and her daughter Lakshmi who is now studying in school.

They and their friends around Gollahalli join me in thanking you for making
these milestones possible.

With best wishes,

Sister Celestine.

The following extracts are from the collectors' booklet of the same year.

This is one small example of the achievements of small, home-grown development projects. Throughout the Third World, projects funded with Christian Aid's grants provide hundreds of thousands of people with access to clean water and adequate food, shelter, health care and education. More importantly, they give people control over their own lives and with it the kind of dignity, choices and opportunities to which human beings have a right.

Prayer

A Christian prayer:

Giver of life, who came that everyone might have life in all its fulness, we pray for those whose lives never reach their full potential because they struggle only to survive; in the name of Jesus who gave his life for all.

Amen

3   And now for the good news

Put a copy of this extract inside a newspaper (preferably 'Christian Aid News') for the first reader to read from. Have at least two readers.

This is taken from an article in *Christian Aid News* in 1991:

To judge by some of the recent outpourings of the British press, there would seem to be little hope for the Third World and little point in supporting its efforts to develop. But I have a message for the prophets of doom: development can and does work.

It is far too easy to be distracted by the disasters and emergencies that make the headlines and to lose sight of the wider picture of what is going on in the Third World. Over the past three decades steady progress has been made in most countries:

    average life expectancy has increased by 16 years;
    adult literacy by 40 per cent;
    and nutritional levels by over 20 per cent per person;
    child mortality rates have been halved.
In other words, developing countries have taken just over 30 years to achieve what took nearly a century in the industrialised countries.

Africa is widely perceived as the continent of wars, famine, AIDS, perpetual crisis and little else. Yet throughout the length and breadth of the continent peasant movements are springing up, mobilising millions of families to improve their livelihoods, look after the environment and provide their own health, education and even postal services. The same can be witnessed in much of Latin America and Asia, yet we do not see it. The positive reality of people working hard to do better is not captured by our mass media.

(*'Christian Aid News', July/September, 1991, article by Tony Hill*)

The article goes on to say that, rather than stop giving, we should stop taking. The low prices we pay in our supermarkets for tea and coffee, for example, are closely linked to the low wages paid to poor farmers. A Sri Lankan woman earns only 10 pence for plucking enough tea leaves to provide 100 cups of tea in Britain. The money governments give in aid to developing countries is often tied to what they are prepared to import from the donor countries in return. When poor countries are given loans to help them develop, they are often crippled by paying the high rate of interest on the loans.

The writer of the article sees signs of hope, particularly in the recognition that you cannot *make* people develop – it must be the people themselves who take charge of their own development. Yet we can stand beside them and support them in their struggle.

Prayer

We belong to the world community,
to all that is good and all that is bad in it.
Help us to play our part,
to take our share of responsibility,
that we may laugh and cry together.

Amen

(*'A World Together', Christian Aid leaflet for use with young people*)

SAVE THE CHILDREN

Save the Children ⫯

1 Aims

Display the charity's logo.
Use different speakers, suitably positioned, for each of the starred sections.

Save the Children is another of the major aid agencies working in the developing countries and in the UK. As its name suggests, it has a particular concern for the welfare of children. Save the Children works directly with children and young people, or with their families and communities, and with other organisations and governments. The experience it has gained over the years means that its voice is respected by the public and officialdom, so that it can influence policy in favour of the needs and rights of children worldwide.

This is how Save the Children describes its work:

★ Famine continues to threaten the lives of countless Africans so Save the Children has stepped up emergency relief. It is also working to enable people to withstand future food crises.

★ Every year 14 million children under five die from preventable diseases. Save the Children is working to meet the health needs of mothers and children by building the capacity of governments to provide accessible, appropriate and affordable health care.

★ There are over 17 million refugees worldwide, half of them children. Save the Children is delivering relief and seeking long-term improvements through reforms in the international system for the care and protection of refugees.

82

★ Orphans, child victims of war, street children and children with disabilities – Save the Children continues to meet the needs of children robbed of their childhood by violence, poverty and exploitation.

★ Unemployment, low income, poor housing and social isolation can mean parents are unable to provide for their children as they would like to. Save the Children supports families through community-based child care projects.

★ Young people are on the receiving end of a system which often fails to listen or learn from young citizens. By heeding what young people have to say about their lives and hopes and supporting their action to bring about change, Save the Children is helping them to secure their rights.

★ When children are in prison it can lock them into a life of crime. When parents are in prison, children serve sentences of discrimination, financial hardship and family breakdown. Save the Children is pressing for replacement to custody schemes for young people and addressing the needs of prisoners' families.

(Selected from the 'Save the Children Review', 1992)

Prayer

We all love babies and little children, and couldn't bear to see them hurt. Sadly, for families in need, it is often the children who suffer most, not least because they don't understand why it is happening to them, and because they cannot protect themselves. We pray for all who have care of little children. May God grant them patience, energy, good humour and common sense.

Amen

2   Voice of the children

Use pupils for this assembly. Position them in different parts of the hall for the starred sections.

★ All children should be given a good education, regardless of class, sex, race or religion.

★ We would like jobs when we leave school, not just training schemes with no promise of a job at the end.

★ People with disabilities should have the same chances in life as everybody else.

★ Public transport should be better, cheaper and more efficient, to encourage people to leave their cars at home.

★ Animals have as much right to live on this earth as we do. Ban all blood sports. Make sure that everything sold in shops is cruelty-free.

★ We want all countries to join together to provide more food and aid for the poorer countries around the world. They should not be exploited by the richer countries.

★ All nuclear and chemical weapons should be banned. The money should then be spent on saving the planet instead.

Imagine a BBC *Any Questions* but with all the questions coming from children and young people. In 1992 Children's Hearings were held in many countries around the world as part of an international 'Voice of the Children' initiative. Save the Children along with UNICEF and the Worldwide Fund for Nature sponsored the Children's Hearings in the UK.

First came the quickfire volley of issues: environmental pollution, young homelessness, women's rights and childcare. Then came the facts to back them up. And that was only the questions! No wonder the adults under fire seemed a little unnerved – they obviously hadn't expected such sustained and reasoned questioning by 'children'. Audience participation became lively – once adults in the audience had been told to pipe down! Other questions leapt from concerns about meeting EC drinking water standards to young people's need for advice about drug problems . . . and much more.

The children of today will soon be running the world of tomorrow. We need access to knowledge and information if we are going to make our world a better place to live in. And we want our voice to be heard.

(*'World's Children', Summer 1992*)

Prayer

Let us think for a moment about the issues that concern *us* most . . . Choose the two which are most important to you . . . What more can you do to find out about these issues? . . . What more can you do to get other people involved? . . . What more can you do to support organisations which are already doing something about it? . . .

Soon the world will be in *our* hands. May we be ready to take care of it, so that we can pass on a better world to *our* children.

Amen

3   Street wise

Display the charity's logo.
Use a variety of speakers.
You could construct a shelter made from cardboard boxes, to illustrate how some street dwellers live.

Street children – they could be in London, Rio, or almost any large city in the world. There are an estimated 100 million of them.

In Britain, research shows that most young people picked up on the street have had problems at home or in care, including violence, abuse or simply being told to leave. Over half are under 16. Young people especially from Northern England, Scotland and Ireland are drawn to the cities by the bright lights and the prospect of work.

Most street children are in Latin America, particularly Brazil, but increasingly their numbers are growing in Africa and Asia. They may be orphans, runaways or refugees. Many sleep at home but earn their living on the streets. Some whole families live on the streets. Some children become members of street gangs and learn to fend for themselves. In Brazil, most people come to live on the streets through sheer poverty: many have come to the city centres from sprawling shanty towns where poor education, overcrowding and lack of jobs lead them to try to make a better life elsewhere.

Here in Britain we rely on the police, social services and voluntary agencies to provide emergency accommodation and counselling. In Brazil the problem is much greater. Here nearly 8 million children survive on the streets by shining shoes, selling on the black market, begging or stealing. Many get dragged into the underworld of drugs and prostitution. As if that wasn't enough, a research institute in Rio estimated that in 1990 alone, 457 children in Brazil were exterminated by death squads in an effort to 'clean up' the city's streets.

(Autumn 1991, 'Youth Topics', Christian Aid, CAFOD, SCIAF)

In Sri Lanka, more and more families appear on the streets of Colombo, driven there by extreme poverty and hopes of employment. Save the Children runs playgroups for these children, gives vocational training to the teenagers, and has day centres which care for children while their mothers go out to work.

Ranjanie is just one child who has benefited, so that she can now look forward to a more worthwhile future than living on the streets. Ranjanie is 12 and lives with her family on the streets of Colombo. She has two sisters and a brother. The family keeps its limited belongings under a plastic sheet to shield them from the rain – they still get wet. Up until a year ago Ranjanie had never been to school. But with the literacy classes provided by Save the Children she was able to catch up with schoolchildren of her age. She now attends the local school and her ambition is to become a teacher. And soon she and her family will no longer have to worry about their things getting wet. They will soon get a house through the intervention of Save the Children.

Prayer

Lord, there may be times when some of us feel like running away from home. We may feel that no-one understands us or has time for us, or that life could be more exciting elsewhere. Please help us through these difficult times. Help us to appreciate the security of our homes and schools. And help us to find someone to talk to about our feelings.

Amen

LEPRA

1 Leprosy

Use different voices for each new paragraph, either by alternating readers or by using six different readers.

There are some illnesses we rarely hear about today, but which were still feared in our grandparents' day. Illnesses like polio and diphtheria came in epidemics and were killers. Special hospitals which were built for the many TB patients have now been converted for other medical uses. We have controlled these illnesses through immunisation programmes – as you will know if you're in Year 9, when TB vaccinations are done!

Another illness that has been controlled in this country is leprosy. Leprosy was widespread in Europe in the Middle Ages but the last time someone caught it in Britain was about 200 years ago. But leprosy hasn't died out. There are still some cases of it in the USA, Spain and parts of eastern Europe; and there are 9 million people suffering from it worldwide, a third of whom live in India. There *are* still some leprosy patients in Britain – about 300 of them – but these have all caught the disease while living abroad.

We have not eradicated leprosy through vaccinations but through better general health care and better living standards. It thrives where there is poor hygiene, overcrowded living conditions and poor nutrition. It is therefore most widespread today in the developing countries of Africa, Latin America and Asia.

So we are unlikely to come across people with leprosy unless we travel abroad to developing countries. There, leprosy sufferers may be recognised by the disfigurements caused by the disease such as nodules on the face, claw hands or club hands and feet. Leprosy is caused by a small germ which attacks the nerves of the extremities of the body. When a sufferer has lost any feeling in his fingers and toes it is easy to damage them without realising it, especially in countries where people go about in bare feet and cook over open fires. Constant damage to hands and feet can wear away the bones, and ulcers can eat away at the body tissue, eventually leaving only stubs. The disease can also cause blindness by nerve damage to the eyelid. Leprosy itself does not kill, but it can leave the sufferer disabled and weak, unable to resist other diseases which may kill them.

Contrary to popular opinion, leprosy is *not* highly contagious. In fact there are two types of leprosy. The more common form is not infectious and develops only slowly because sufferers have some degree of natural resistance. The more serious form spreads more rapidly and does become infectious, the germ probably being passed on by droplets in the air from nasal secretions

Prayer

Let us imagine for a few moments what it must be like to lose the sense of feeling in our hands. How would we tell the temperature of the water for our morning wash? It would be easy to burn our hands without knowing it. How would we know if we cut ourselves on the bread-knife, or caught our fingers in a kitchen drawer? How would we know if we had frost-bite in the cold weather? How would we know how much strength to exert when lifting things?

We can understand how easy it is for leprosy sufferers to damage their hands once they have lost the feeling in them, and sympathise with the panic they must feel as they see their hands and feet becoming more and more useless. Look now at your own hands . . . Turn them over . . . Feel them . . . Clench and unclench your fists, and give thanks for them.

Amen

2 LEPRA'S work

Use a number of readers.

Leprosy is a disease which attacks the nerves and which, if left untreated, can cause horrible deformity of the hands, feet and face.

The good news is that leprosy can be cured by multidrug therapy. This cures the milder form of leprosy within six months and most of the more serious cases within two years. It also makes patients non-infectious, so that they can be treated in their own homes.

The bad news is that, of the estimated 12 million sufferers in 1991 only 2 million of these were receiving treatment.

If leprosy can be cured, why are so many people still suffering from it?

Leprosy is most common in the poorest countries of the world. These countries cannot afford comprehensive programmes of leprosy control; in fact it is often difficult for people to get to a doctor when medical services are so thin on the ground. Meanwhile the leprosy germs continue to thrive in unhealthy living conditions and to attack people with low resistance because of poor diets.

This is why LEPRA exists – The British Leprosy Relief Association. It was founded in 1924 with the clear aim of helping to control and eventually eradicate leprosy. In 1990, almost 20,000 leprosy patients were cured on LEPRA-supported programmes in nine different countries, including India, Ethiopia and Brazil.

The effectiveness of LEPRA's work can be seen in the African country of Malawi. Twenty five years ago the Government of Malawi asked LEPRA to help them organise a national leprosy control programme. Since then the number of leprosy cases has been reduced from 50,000 to 2,000. It costs LEPRA just £45 to send a team into a Malawi school to examine up to 500 children and provide treatment for those who need it. It is in Malawi that LEPRA is trialling a vaccine against leprosy, the results of which are not yet known; and it continues to fund research into treatment of the disease.

At one school in Malawi, 300 children were screened and only one 12 year old boy was found to have leprosy. Luckily for George, his leprosy was caught at an early stage before he had suffered any loss of feeling or disablement. He will be completely cured. When the leprosy team visited his home to explain to his parents about the disease and the drug treatment, they discovered that his 21 year old sister also had leprosy, and were able to treat her too. The rest of the family, and the whole village, were screened for leprosy and cleared.

(*'LEPRA Today'*, *adapted*)

Prayer

Lord, it is shameful that people are suffering from leprosy who could be cured. May we be indignant at such injustice, and may our indignation lead us to *do* something on their behalf.

Amen

3 Two famous leprosy workers

Use three readers for the three sections here.

Some of you may have heard of Father Damien. He was a monk and priest who went as a missionary to the islands of Hawaii and Molokai. He is famous for his work among leprosy sufferers there.

In 1873 he asked to be sent to live among them, knowing that he would not be allowed to come back because the colony where they lived was a place of quarantine where those who suffered from this dreadful disease could be kept apart from other people. In those days there was no cure for leprosy and people were very frightened of this disease. Father Damien worked single-handed to minister to the needs of the leprosy sufferers. As the only able-bodied person in the leprosy colony, he dressed their wounds, built their houses and dug their graves, as well as being their priest.

One day, he accidentally spilt some boiling water on himself, but he felt no pain. At that moment he knew that *he* had contracted leprosy, but he continued his work as long as he could, now being able to identify himself fully with the people whom he served. He died there in 1889 at the age of 49.

That was over a hundred years ago. But Professor Jagadisan died only recently, in 1991, at the age of 82. He too contracted leprosy, and he too has won international fame for devoting his life to helping those who suffer from this disease.

Jagadisan developed leprosy when he was only ten years old, but it was the non-infectious type and he was able to finish his studies. He gained a degree in English and taught for 11 years. Then came the turning point in his life when he was refused a college lectureship because of his leprosy. This made him decide to spend the rest of his life fighting the prejudice that exists against leprosy sufferers. He realised that people needed to be educated about this disease. He started by working for the Indian branch of LEPRA which at that time was known as the British Empire Leprosy Relief Association, and took an important role when the Indian branch of this organisation became independent. He travelled the length and breadth of the huge subcontinent of India, vetting requests for support, and showing particular concern for the children who suffered from leprosy. He was a known authority on leprosy at international conferences and much sought after as a writer and speaker on this subject.

Jagadisan could not have done his work with such sympathy for leprosy sufferers if he had not been one himself. He courageously fought against the prejudice that people like himself had to suffer, and proved that people with leprosy can still lead fulfilling and worthwhile lives. Although the disease gradually made life more difficult for him, he lived to a ripe old age.

Prayer

We have heard of two people who have known at first hand what it is to suffer from leprosy, and who have used this experience to help others. We give thanks for the human spirit which can rise above the physical disabilities and social stigma of leprosy. Help us to learn from Father Damien and Professor Jagadisan how to turn misfortune to good effect in the service of others.

Amen

4 The fear of leprosy

There are a number of sections here, for up to five readers.

One reason why leprosy is still widespread is poverty. Another reason is fear and superstition. Leprosy can disfigure people very badly, it can be contagious, and up until recently there was no cure for it, therefore, people have been very frightened of this disease. When leprosy was detected, the sufferer used to be sent away from his or her village, and sufferers would live together in colonies. When they travelled around they would ring bells to warn other people to keep away.

It is important to diagnose leprosy in the early stages before it has done any harm to the nerves or caused disablement. The drugs can stop the disease, but it cannot put back fingers and toes; and physiotherapy can only have a limited success in bringing back into use claw hands and drop feet. But many people are afraid to go for help when they see early warnings of the disease. They hope they are mistaken and that it will go away. They pull their clothes over the tell-tale white patches of skin which have lost their feeling, and only admit to having the disease years later when it is too advanced to hide. Regular screening programmes in schools are one way of detecting the illness early in children.

Modern drugs can now cure leprosy and make it non-infectious so that patients can be treated in their own homes. But there is still a lot of ignorance and fear of the disease – just as there is in this country of AIDS – and many patients still have to go away to hospitals and clinics for treatment, because their families and neighbours are too frightened to keep them at home. It will take a long time before people treat leprosy like any other illness. Education programmes are going on in schools so that young people grow up knowing that leprosy can be cured.

One boy who suffered from people's prejudice against leprosy is Asmat, a ten year old Indian boy, who is being helped by LEPRA, a charity for leprosy sufferers.

Asmat was very keen to help during filming in the city of Hyderabad and LEPRA staff were so taken by his bright, bubbly personality that he ended up as the star of a special version of the film made for schools.

Asmat has had leprosy for about two years. He had just finished his first year at school when the disease began to affect his right foot, leaving him with a pronounced limp.

The fear and superstition still associated with leprosy forced Asmat to leave school and led his family to move home. Since then he has been working with both his mother and his sister in a chewing gum factory – 8 hours a day, 6 days a week, for which he earns 4.5 rupees (that is just 12 pence) a day.

Asmat was referred to LEPRA workers when he began to have problems with his foot. He was put on treatment and has been provided with a special sandal. His foot is now beginning to improve. Because he has the more serious form of the disease, he will need treatment for another 18 months, and then his cure should be complete.
(*LEPRA News, No 73*)

Prayer

Lord, we pray that, when we come across people who are sick, or handicapped, or elderly, we may have compassion greater than the fear or awkwardness we may feel. And we pray that good sense will overcome any prejudices we may have towards them, so that our attitudes or thoughtlessness do not add to their suffering.

Amen

THE TERRENCE HIGGINS TRUST

1   Jesus touched the leper

Use at least two readers, to emphasise the change from considering biblical leprosy to present day AIDS.

Some of us may only have heard of leprosy from the Bible and our knowledge and views of it may, therefore, be rather old fashioned.

In the Old Testament there are detailed laws concerning the treatment of leprosy sufferers, which show the need in those days to isolate people with contagious diseases:

The person with such an infectious disease must wear torn clothes, let his hair be unkempt, cover the lower part of his face and cry out, 'Unclean! Unclean!'. As long as he has the infection he remains unclean. He must live alone; he must live outside the camp.
(Leviticus 13:45–46)

These laws still applied in New Testament times when Jesus lived. Yet he set an example of how to treat people who were suffering, both physically from their illness and also by being shunned by society. The story is told very briefly in Mark's Gospel, but notice what Jesus does to the man with leprosy.

A man with leprosy came to him and begged him on his knees, 'If you are willing, you can make me clean.'

Filled with compassion, Jesus reached out his hand and touched the man. 'I am willing,' he said. 'Be clean!' Immediately the leprosy left him and he was cured.
(Mark 1:40–42)

The significant thing in this incident, apart from the miraculous cure, is that Jesus reached out his hand and touched the man. While other people were keeping their distance for fear of catching the dreaded disease, Jesus showed his concern for this fellow human being by making physical contact with him.

The stigma which is now associated with HIV and AIDS is similar to the age-old stigma associated with leprosy. Jesus' example encourages us to see that, behind frightening words like 'AIDS', there are real people like you and me who need sympathy and help. Surely their discovery of being HIV positive, or the physical pain that AIDS brings is enough, without adding to their suffering by our ignorance and prejudice.

Eva Heymann works with the Family Support Network of the Terrence Higgins Trust, and is only too aware of the threats and abuse that families of AIDS sufferers are often subjected to. She tells of how, the morning after the funeral of a boy with haemophilia, the family woke up to find graffiti on their house, saying 'AIDS is here'. Another example she gives is when a 6 year old twin child died of AIDS and the family received poisoned phone calls insisting that the other twin was removed from school. This family had to be rehoused.

Eva was born in Germany and, as a Jew, she herself experienced all the horrors of being shunned, marginalised and outcast during the War. After arriving in the UK as a refugee she became a nun and now counsels families affected by the HIV virus. Despite the appalling examples of cruelty that she has given above, she believes there is now a swing to a much more compassionate response to AIDS sufferers, as people are better educated about this illness.

Prayer

Lord, help us to reach out to people who are shunned by our society. We think particularly of the thousands of people suffering from AIDS in this country – men, women and children from all sections of society.

Amen

2   A friend in need

Use at least two readers.

The latest statistics from the Department of Health confirm that HIV and AIDS are now very real problems for all sections of Britain's population. More and more people desperately need help. The Terrence Higgins Trust is the best known charity in this country for people who have been diagnosed as HIV positive and those with AIDS. Their aim is to inform, advise and help on AIDS and HIV infection.

In 1987 the Trust had only a few members of staff. By 1991 it had over a thousand workers, mostly unpaid volunteers. They are on the end of a telephone line, offering understanding and knowledgeable advice, to 400 callers a week. Callers may be perfectly well but worried that they could have been infected by the HIV virus. People who are HIV positive or have AIDS usually need legal advice. Some need to come for sessions with a counsellor. Some need financial assistance from the Hardship Fund or practical help. Volunteers know how important that first telephone call is and are taught that no effort is too much.

There is a saying 'A friend in need is a friend indeed' and another important aspect of this charity's work is to befriend people who have AIDS in their time of need, often when their own friends and families have rejected them. This is done by volunteers who are trained for it and are called Buddys. A person with AIDS can ask to have a Buddy who will understand how HIV and AIDS can affect people and who will be there to give the friendship and support needed for the person with AIDS to carry on with his or her life.

Prayer

'A friend in need is a friend indeed.'

True friends stick by you when you need them. They won't let you down when things get tough.

Friends accept you as you are. You don't need to pretend with them.

You can trust your friends with your secrets, your confidences, your private thoughts.

Friends understand you; they know how you feel; they sympathise with you. When you're in need, a real friend is there, always ready to listen and to give support.

Let us give thanks for our friends . . . name them in your mind . . .
Let us pray that we may be good friends in return . . .
And pray for people who find it difficult to make friends . . .

Amen

3 Ultimate concerns

Be sensitive to anyone in the audience who has recently been bereaved. This is best read by an adult.

At some time or other in our lives all of us are brought up against important issues or events that put other things into perspective for us. It is quite common for people who are going through bereavement to begin to question their own beliefs and values. They begin to wonder if work and money are really that important compared to relationships with those they love. Sometimes we only really appreciate people when we have lost them. And it may only be when the certainty of death is brought home to us, that we begin to really value the gift of life.

AIDS is like a death sentence hanging over many young lives. One person who has AIDS writes:

'I'm sorry, but I'm afraid you are HIV positive.'
I can't remember the exact words my doctor used to break the news, panic had already deafened me. And the word AIDS was ringing round my brain – even though it hadn't been mentioned.'
(Newsletter from Martyn Taylor, 1991)

In situations like this, people are forced to take stock. 50 per cent of people who are diagnosed HIV positive have gone on to develop AIDS – for which, at the moment, there is no cure. Sufferers lose their resistance to other diseases which eventually kill them.

Yet, in a newsletter from the Terrence Higgins Trust, the Chair of the Board of Directors said this:

Some people I know with AIDS say it is the best thing that has happened to them. It's not a thought I share, but I can see why they say it. It's because of the way this place often brings out the best in people, motivating them to achieve quite extraordinary results. There's a vitality in it all. Constantly we hear inspiring stories of great personal courage and tales of immense dignity and love.
(1991)

When people have nothing more to lose, when they know they have a limited time to live, they are free to value things of real worth in life: friendship, courage and love.

Prayer

Lord, don't let us wait for some tragedy to make us take stock of our lives. Help us, now, to be thankful for the gift of life and to make the most of it. Help us to realise the importance of our relationships with family and friends, and not to be afraid to tell and show people that we care for them.

Amen

THE CHILDREN'S SOCIETY

1　No fooling

This could be done by three readers: the last taking the final paragraph and the prayer. Readers may be prepared to wear jester's hats (which can be made from cardboard – instructions on p. 126).

On the front cover of *Gateway*, the magazine of The Children's Society, was a picture of Russ Abbot, dressed as a court jester. It was the Spring '92 edition, and this well-loved comedian was launching a special appeal for the Society, to start on 1 April – April Fool's Day. Russ Abbot's aim was to put the fun back into fundraising, and for 12 days around the country zany happenings took place: funny walk competitions, giant open-air congas, a custard pie rally, and much more. Children and adults from all walks of life took part – wearing yellow, red and blue jester's hats with bells on them, in an effort to raise money for The Children's Society.

Inside the magazine we are asked to 'spare *jester* little time to help bring smiles to the faces of thousands of children, young people and their families'. For The Children's Society works with over 11,000 children, young people and their families through 160 projects across England and Wales. The range of work is tremendous. The Society started out as the Church of England's Central Home for Waifs and Strays. In 1945 it was renamed the Church of England's Children's Society, and was known for its work as an adoption agency and in running children's homes. Now it also runs 55 Family Centres which provide a safety valve for families living under the severe strain of poverty and disadvantage. It was the first organisation to open safe houses offering refuge for young runaways. It supports projects to help young people get on their feet, including a youth training project which helps pregnant teenage girls among others. Its voice is heard wherever children in this country are in need; and its workers are there for children with disabilities who need placing in a loving family, for abused children who need representing in court, and for young people in trouble with the police.

Childhood should be full of fun and laughter and happy memories. Tragically, for many children the world is a brutal place. The Children's

Society exists for such children. Its aim is to help children develop to their full potential in a caring and positive environment.

Prayer

Let us think of some of the people who make us laugh – our favourite TV comedians – friends – members of our family – teachers even! We give thanks for the human capacity to laugh and have fun. We pray for children and young people who, for whatever reason, are finding it difficult to smile and laugh at the moment.

Amen

2 Fostering and adoption

This could be shared between a number of readers.

Emma, aged four, is confined to a wheelchair, fed by tube and will never be able to speak. She knows no different. From birth her brain failed to develop normally, her muscles were deformed and her senses impaired – the doctors diagnosed cerebral palsy. Her parents were devastated. They loved Emma but felt they couldn't cope, and at the age of 18 months she was taken into local authority care. Her future seemed uncertain.

The Children's Society Family Placement Project helps find loving homes for children like Emma who are difficult to place. When Jenny Nichols, the project leader, heard about Emma, she thought of the Mathie family. Alan and Angela Mathie had three children of their own, had been fostering young people with disabilities for two years, and were now keen to adopt. Before any adoption goes ahead the Society workers make sure that the potential parents will be able to meet the needs of the child. For six months Alan and Angela met with Emma while their suitability was assessed by social workers and doctors. And at the end of that time, Emma found herself with two new sisters, a brother and loving parents.

Since moving in with the Mathies, the change in Emma has been remarkable. The medical report painted a bleak picture, but it was not long before Emma started to respond to family life, as Angela explains:

After staying with us a very short time we noticed that Emma was taking things in and making eye contact – progress has been slow, but it's worth it. Now she reacts just as any other 4 year old would, shouting for attention, always smiling and giggling and she gets on with my other 3 children fantastically. Emma is adorable and we all love her to bits!

And what about Emma's natural parents? The project ensures that links are maintained with them. Just because they couldn't cope, it does not mean that they do not love their daughter, and in future they may be able to help. Angela writes and sends them photographs twice a year, informing them of Emma's progress and keeping the lines of communication open.

(*'Gateway', Winter 1991*)

Prayer

We pray for all parents who have had to give up their children – who have made this supreme sacrifice because they knew their children would be better cared for by someone else.

We pray for foster parents and adoptive parents – who have this enormous capacity to love other people's children like their own.

We pray especially for people like Alan and Angela Mathie, whose lives are now spent changing Emma's nappies, getting up in the middle of the night for her, and seeing to her every need.

May the Lord bless them all, grant them inner strength and the joy of knowing that they are doing their best for the children.

Amen

THE SPASTICS SOCIETY

1 What's in a name?

This is probably best read by an adult since the vocabulary is quite complicated at times.

The Spastics Society was founded back in 1952 by a group of parents with children who had cerebral palsy. The Spastics Society is now the largest national charity working with adults and children with cerebral palsy, and is giving support and advice to thousands of people across England and Wales.

Every year in Britain more than 1,500 babies are born with cerebral palsy. On average a baby with cerebral palsy is born once in every 400 births. It is not usually inherited: it can happen in any family regardless of sex, race or social background. Yet most people know very little about this physical disability which affects so many lives.

Cerebral palsy is a physical disability caused by an injury to the brain which occurs before birth, at birth or during a child's early years. A part of the brain is affected which controls movement and posture and this results in varying degrees of disability. No two people with cerebral palsy are the same. It's as individual as people themselves. It is often assumed that people who cannot control their facial expressions have a mental disability. But some people with cerebral palsy have higher than average intelligence, whilst others have severe learning difficulties.

The Spastics Society retains its original name because it is so well known by that name, but it dislikes the use of the term 'Spastics' for people with spastic and other types of cerebral palsy. It is particularly insensitive to refer to people as if they actually *are* the condition that they are affected by. This dehumanises them. No-one refers to people with cancer as 'cancerites' for example.

The Spastics Society is trying to educate the general public into having a better attitude towards people with cerebral palsy. You may have seen their advertisements with the message 'Our biggest handicap is other people's attitudes'. And just think about the radio-programme for people with disabilities which is called *Does he take sugar?* because, so often, we assume that they can't answer for themselves. People with cerebral palsy don't want our sympathy, they need practical help to achieve fulfilling lives.

The Spastics Society tries to work in partnership with people who have cerebral palsy, enabling them as far as possible to run their own lives and to achieve their aims and goals in life. It gives specialised education in its schools and colleges for children as young as two through to young adults of 19. It also runs residential units and work centres. It gives advice through its specialist social workers, careers advisers and advisers on sports and leisure activities. It also supports research into the causes and effects of cerebral palsy – though we still don't understand exactly why or how it happens. It also actively campaigns in Parliament to make sure that the concerns of people with disabilities are heard and reflected in the laws.

(Material taken from leaflets produced by The Spastics Society)

Prayer

Let us try to be honest with ourselves – when we see a person in a wheelchair do we see the person or the wheelchair? When we see someone severely disabled by cerebral palsy, do we pity them or befriend them as we would any one else? Help us, Lord, to see the person rather than the disability.

Amen

2   Independence

To be read by senior pupils.

As we grow up, we gain more and more independence, and we look forward to the time when we are adults and can run our own lives. The same is true for people who grow up with physical disabilities – they want to get jobs, get married, have a home of their own just like everyone else, but they need more help to achieve their aims in life. The Spastics Society believes that every individual has a right to control his or her own life and to share in the opportunities, enjoyment, challenges and responsibilities of everyday life. The Society exists to help people with cerebral palsy overcome their disabilities and wherever possible it encourages them to integrate into the normal community rather than become institutionalised.

Bob is a good example of this. He is 40 years old and spent a lot of his life in a Spastics Society residential centre. Then he had the opportunity to move into a specially adapted bungalow in the grounds where, for two years, he was helped to learn the skills needed to live independently: to dress himself, cook and go shopping. These everyday tasks are very demanding for Bob who finds it hard to control his body movements. Now Bob's lifelong dream has come true and he is living in his own home. He has also started at college and is making new friends.

Nikki is a pretty 20 year old. When she first came to a Spastics Society school she was unable to walk or speak. Now she communicates through a simple device called a Word Board and, like many young people nowadays, she has learned to use a computer. Nikki still finds communication hard work but says 'I will not give in 'til I have got the message across!' The latest news from Nikki is that she is on a training course which is helping her to develop vocational skills so that she can get a job.

People with cerebral palsy are helped to do all kinds of sports and leisure activities, including daring things like rock climbing. We see them on television taking part in marathons; and they compete in their wheelchairs in the Paralympic Games which run parallel to the Olympic Games.

The Society is now encouraging more integration between people with physical handicaps and the able-bodied, from a much younger age.

Nursery schools are planned which have the facilities for disabled children but can also take non-disabled children. And special units, staffed by the Society, are attached to mainstream schools so that we can all grow up together.

(Taken from a pamphlet produced by The Spastics Society 1992)

Prayer

We all have disabilities of one sort or another; and we are all gifted in some way. One person may have an attractive personality, but may not be very strong. Another person may be physically very fit, but may not find academic subjects very easy. Not everyone can swim, or drive a car, however many lessons they have had. Even those who seem to have everything going for them may not be entirely happy with themselves and their lives.

Lord, you love each of us just as we are. Help us to accept ourselves, with all our imperfections, and to accept other people with theirs. Help us to see the good in ourselves and the good in others. Help us to see people with disabilities as *people*, just like the rest of us.

Amen

FRIENDS OF THE EARTH

Friends of the Earth

1   Twenty-one today

Display the Friends of the Earth logo.
For best effect, use a different reader for each starred section and
illustrate each issue e.g. with large cardboard cut-outs of a bottle, a tiger,
a whale etc. – or with the real thing e.g. a bottle, a fur coat, a glass of
drinking water etc.

In 1992 Friends of the Earth celebrated its 21st birthday, marking over
two decades of campaigning to protect the environment. It began in
Britain but is now represented (as Friends of the Earth International) in
47 countries across every continent. It has over 500,000 supporters
worldwide.

★ Friends of the Earth hit the headlines for the first time in May 1971
when it returned 2,000 non-returnable bottles to the London
headquarters of Cadbury Schweppes. This simple action received
excellent media coverage and brought both the returnable bottle issue
and the name of Friends of the Earth to the attention of the British public
for the first time.

★ In the early days one of its main concerns was the protection of
endangered wildlife. In 1972 it launched a campaign to persuade people
not to buy tiger, leopard and cheetah furs. Its lobbying led to the 1976
import ban on the skins of these endangered species.

★ Throughout the 1970s its 'Save the Whale' campaign was a significant
factor behind the 1982 European Community's decision to ban imports of
whale products.

★ The 1980s saw the Wildlife Campaign move in a new direction, towards the conservation of habitats, rather than individual species. This has continued into the 1990s, with its campaign to protect Britain's peatlands. Many garden centres and superstores nationwide have agreed to promote alternatives to peat.

★ Its Acid Rain Campaign was launched in 1984 when its survey of beech and yew trees in England and Wales revealed that more than half were suffering ill effects from acid rain.

★ Since the discovery of the hole in the ozone layer in 1984, Friends of the Earth has kept up pressure to ban CFCs and other chemicals which destroy the ozone layer.

★ Since 1989 Friends of the Earth has also been a watchdog on the quality of our drinking water, and has forced the government to bring forward its deadline for removing pesticides from the water supplied to millions of consumers.
(*Take and adapted from 'Earth Matters', Issue Number 14*)

These are but a few of Friends of the Earth's successes. It continues to work on local, national and international campaigns, bringing environmental issues to the public notice and so putting pressure on those in government who have the power to bring about change. It has helped to make 'green issues' fashionable, and has affected many of the products on our supermarket shelves.

Prayer

Lord, help *us* to be friends of the earth:
friends of the earth in the way we shop;
friends of the earth in the way we use the earth's precious resources;
friends of the earth in our defence of the great diversity of plant and
animal species and their natural environments;
friends of the earth in the influence we can bring to bear on business-
people and politicians,
so that they take seriously environmental issues.

Amen

2   Global warming

Display the Friends of the Earth logo.
The first section should be delivered as a stirring speech.
The rest falls naturally into sections for a number of readers.

Distinguished delegates. I hold in my hand a time bomb. *(Hold aloft a model of the world.)* . . . You cannot run away and leave it to explode in someone else's face. Instead, it needs facing up to with determination and resolve . . .

Global warming is such a time bomb: ready to explode, unless we take action now.
(*'Special Report'*, *published by UNA youth & students*)

This was part of the speech delivered by 14-year-old Joanna Reyes and 17-year-old Ralph Wilde at the United Nations Second World Climate Conference in Geneva in 1990. They were the youth ambassadors chosen by the United Nations Association to speak to ministers at the conference from all over the world. They were voicing a concern that many of us feel.

A hole was discovered by British scientists in the ozone layer over the Antarctic back in 1984. In 1988 NASA confirmed that the ozone situation was worse than we had thought; and the next year a hole over the Arctic was discovered as well. Despite pressure on governments and some limitation of the use of CFC gases, by 1991 US scientists announced that the depletion of the ozone layer was occurring twice as fast as they had thought – with serious effects on the health of human beings, animals and plant life.

(*'Ozone Destruction'*, *a leaflet published by Friends of the Earth, 1992*)

Robert Swann is the first person in history to have walked to the North and South Poles – and he has experienced at first hand what we are doing to our planet. Since 1987 he has devoted his energies to drawing attention to the world's environmental crisis. He says:

My team and I walked right under the hole in the ozone layer for months. We didn't know it was there, we couldn't see or feel it, but our flesh burned on our faces. Our skin peeled for months afterwards. Nothing like this had ever happened to polar explorers before.

I'm horrified to learn that sheep in Chile have been blinded by cataracts and off the Falkland Islands fishermen have been catching blind fish! . . .

The problem is that many people, and some of our leaders, haven't yet realised what we already know – that the time to take action is now – before it's too late.
(*From 'The Earth is in Environmental Crisis', UNA, 1992*)

Friends of the Earth has been one of the organisations that, from the beginning, has tirelessly campaigned against this threat to our planet. It was Friends of the Earth which started a massive consumer campaign which brought to an end the use of CFC gases in over 90 per cent of all aerosols and fast-food packaging. In 1987, its boycott threat persuaded McDonalds to stop using CFC-produced packaging; and public awareness has led to the development of ozone-friendly products.

Now Friends of the Earth is stepping up its campaign against ozone-destroying chemicals. It asks why Britain is trailing behind other European countries like Germany in limiting the use of CFCs. It asks why 97 per cent of CFCs in domestic fridges are released into the atmosphere when the fridges are thrown away, when we have the technology to dispose of the CFCs safely. It asks why some big chemical companies are getting away with producing a new type of ozone destroyer in their aerosols. Friends of the Earth concludes that only government action will force industry to act responsibly – and it is putting pressure on the government to do something about it before it is too late.

Prayer

Lord, the Earth is very beautiful –
help us to appreciate it.
The Earth is very useful –
help us to make use of it, without using it up.
The Earth is very vulnerable –
help us to protect it.
The Earth is full of diverse species, and extinction is for ever –
help us to 'Save the Earth'.

Amen

3   Earth Summit

Display the Friends of the Earth logo.
Use a number of different readers.
*To make this a more active assembly, you could ask your art department
to construct a 'tree of life', and prepare a class to come up with their leaf-
pledges which they could read out as they attach them to the tree.*

The Earth Summit took place in Rio de Janeiro, Brazil over 11 days in
June 1992. Its full title was the United Nations Conference on
Environment and Development. Its aim was to form a plan of action to
tackle the interlinked problems of world poverty and pollution.

Attended by over a hundred heads of state, this was the biggest ever
international meeting on the environment and development. It was also
attended by development agencies like Oxfam and Christian Aid, as well
as environmental agencies like Friends of the Earth. They were there to
lobby the politicians. Never before had so many influential leaders been
brought together to tackle these issues. It reflected the level of public
concern with these life and death issues, and was seen by many as our
best chance yet to save our planet.

It may surprise you that the issues of poverty and pollution were seen to
be linked – to be international concerns – and were dealt with at the same
conference. Here are just two examples of how combating poverty and
protecting the environment need to go hand in hand.

★ Although they want to protect their environment, poor people are
forced to cut down trees as their only source of energy. Without the trees,
the soil is eroded and the land becomes less fertile. They also over-use
the land in their attempt to produce enough food to live on, and
eventually the goodness in the soil is used up.

★ But the poor also have a lesson or two to teach the rich about
pollution from waste. Poor people know how to make use of everything.
Many poor people live off other people's rubbish – picking over rubbish
dumps for saleable items like tin cans and waste paper. You don't see
much rubbish on the streets of India, for instance: fresh food is eaten and
put into paper bags made from newspapers – so there is little waste on
packaging; fruit and vegetable peelings are fed to animals; waste paper is
put on the fire. Here in Britain, we throw away 20 million tonnes of

114

rubbish from our homes every year. And although bottle and paper banks are now a familiar sight, still only 3 per cent of our household waste is recycled. Waste not only pollutes our environment – it has to be disposed of somewhere – but it also means that energy is being used up to produce more new things rather than making use of or recycling the old. The mass production, mass consumption and mass disposal of industrialised countries is harming the environment. It is a sobering thought that one United States citizen consumes as much energy as 8,400 citizens of India.

If the development and environment agencies were disappointed by the general lack of definite commitments from the politicians at the Earth Summit, they could not have been disappointed by the response of a million private individuals all over the world who made personal pledges to improve our planet. The frame of a massive 'tree of life' was constructed in Rio where the conference took place, and its cardboard leaves were attached by hundreds of Scouts and Guides. Each leaf had a pledge written on it from its sender to do a little bit to save the earth. British Airways flew in 200,000 pledges from Britain alone.

Prayer

There is a saying about 'turning over a new leaf' to indicate that we want to make a fresh start. The leaf-pledges gave people a chance to make a new effort in connection with the environment and poverty. Think for a moment of what you would like to pledge to do yourself to make this world a better place . . . Lord, help us to take seriously our own part in protecting the environment, both for ourselves and for the poor who are most vulnerable.

Amen

ANIMAL WELFARE

1 Royal Society for the Prevention of Cruelty to Animals

This could be done by one reader, or two readers taking alternative paragraphs.

What would you do if you knew of an animal that was being maltreated, or saw an animal in distress? The right thing to do would be to call the RSPCA. Their inspectors are trained and ready to deal with such calls for help at any time of day or night.

For instance, an RSPCA report from Ashford in Kent tells how some young children found a dog in shock near a busy ring road after a road accident. The dog was injured and was unable to move. Its owners, who must have known the risk of letting the dog out near the road, could not be traced. So the RSPCA treated the dog and is now looking for a new home for him.

In this case, the owners were irresponsible in allowing the dog to get out onto a busy road and in failing to put an identity disc on the dog. Dogs and other animals can suffer from human negligence, like forgetting to walk the dog regularly or feed pets properly. In these cases, people probably don't mean to be cruel to their pets and by simply finding out what their animal needs, suffering can be avoided.

Many owners are irresponsible by allowing their animals to have young without there being enough good homes available. Neutering an animal is a simple operation which will prevent unwanted young being produced and will help reduce the number being abandoned at RSPCA homes.

When we think of cruelty to animals we probably think of criminal cases. Over 2,700 convictions for cruelty to animals were recorded during 1991 alone; and nearly half of these were cases of cruelty to dogs. But thankfully there's a ray of hope in all this. Nearly all of those cases of terrible cruelty were reported to the RSPCA by people who heard or saw something they knew was wrong – and they acted promptly. It shows there are people around who do care what happens to animals. And there are also many people who give money to the RSPCA – the Royal Society for the Prevention of Cruelty to Animals – to support its work in preventing cruelty and promoting kindness to animals.

Prayer

Lord, we give thanks for the privilege of owning pets,
and for the love and companionship they give us.
Help us to care for them willingly and responsibly.
Forgive us if we have ever caused an animal harm.
Make us alert to their cries for help,
and always ready to act on their behalf.

Amen

2   Up for adoption

There are two clear sections here – suitable for two readers.

Many holiday-makers on the Isle of Wight visit its Donkey Sanctuary which, in 1992, was providing a permanent and happy home for nearly 90 donkeys as well as 16 horses and ponies, 3 mules, 25 goats and numerous other small animals. Visitors can stroll around the grassy paddocks where the animals run free, and stroke those donkeys that are not too nervous to come near.

Some of these donkeys have retired after being used for donkey derby rides at seaside resorts. A donkey can live to over 40 years – but their owners often don't want to pay for their keep once their working lives are over. Bruno – a handsome, dark brown heavyweight was a donkey derby animal and is named after that other champion, Frank. Some donkeys are rescued from meat markets, where they are sold for pet-food. Cherry, a nervous dark brown donkey is an example. When she was rescued, she was in foal and has since produced Angel who will be brought up and looked after with Cherry at the Sanctuary.

One way in which money is raised to pay for the Sanctuary is by its 'Adopt a Donkey Scheme'. For an annual subscription of £10 or over, people can choose a particular donkey to support. They are sent a photograph of their donkey and regular newsletters about the Donkey Sanctuary.

This type of 'adoption' is a new way of raising funds for charities. It helps people to feel personally involved and guarantees a regular income. There is even a scheme now to 'Adopt a whale'. A little easier to understand is the 'Adopt a chimp' scheme at Monkey World. This Chimpanzee Rescue Centre in Dorset was featured on TV when Anneka Rice accepted the challenge to get a special quarantine building finished for the chimps when they first arrive from abroad.

Jim Cronin rescued his first four chimps from Spain in 1991. By 1992 there were 30, and he hopes soon to house 50 in his woodland sanctuary in Dorset where the chimps can lead natural lives once more. Under growing pressure on the Spanish authorities, they are now clamping down on the illegal use of live animals as camera props. Remember that holiday

118

in Spain when that cute, dressed-up little chimp clung to you while the photographer snapped your picture? That chimp was probably snatched after its mother was killed by trappers in the jungles of Equatorial Guinea or Senegal. Organised gangs will have sold the baby chimp in Spain where its teeth would be pulled out so that it doesn't bite the tourists. It would be burnt with cigarette ends to make it behave; and by the age of five it would be disposed of, when it gets too big to be cute.

Jim Cronin of Monkey World reminds us that the chimpanzee is the closest living relative to man, yet it is being threatened on all fronts. Habitat destruction, laboratory research, and their use as photographers' props in Spain, if unchecked, will push this amazing creature to the brink of extinction. A chimp at his sanctuary can be adopted by children for £15 per year. They will receive a photograph of the adopted chimpanzee, a certificate and free entry to Monkey World for the period of the adoption.

Prayer

Lord, we give thanks for individuals who care so much about the plight of suffering animals that they refuse to give up the fight until they achieve their goals, and that they are prepared to devote their lives and resources to them. And we give thanks that their commitment stirs the hearts of others to fight alongside them and support them.

Amen

CHARITIES AT CHRISTMAS

1   The Samaritans

Use a number of readers, particularly for the starred sections.

Christmas can make small problems better but big problems worse.

Christmas can often cheer us up and make us forget all the little worries of everyday life. It's a time when classmates make up their quarrels and go around in a group again. It's a time when people blow the expense and splash out on expensive presents. It's a time to stop watching your weight and to enjoy the feasting.

But for many people, their problems are too great to be so easily forgotten. In fact, when they see everyone else enjoying themselves it just makes their own unhappiness seem worse in comparison. There are very many lonely and unhappy people at Christmas:

★ While the rest of us are closing ranks, making arrangements to spend Christmas and Boxing Day and New Year with our families, some people have no families to be with.

★ For people who have been bereaved during the year, Christmas will never be the same again. The pain of their loss is brought back again and again each time they sign a Christmas card and have to remember to leave off their loved one's name.

★ Others will be writing cards early, to let their friends know that their partner has left. Those brief notes hardly begin to convey the misery that such broken relationships entail.

There are very many lonely and unhappy people at Christmastime. Over the Christmas period in 1990 more than 100 people in Britain became so desperate that they took their own lives. They saw no hope in their misery and anguish, and found suicide preferable to the prospect of facing another day.

Thankfully there is an organisation at the end of a telephone for people who are that desperate and feel they have no one else to confide in. This organisation was started in 1953 by Chad Varah, a Church of England priest, and is now well-known. It is called the Samaritans – after the Good Samaritan in the parable Jesus told about loving our neighbours. But, although started by a Christian, the Samaritans is not a religious organisation, and it helps people of any religion or none at all.

The Samaritans have 186 centres up and down the country, open 24 hours a day, every day of the year. People – young and old – can phone or visit them to talk over their problems. They are assured of sympathy and confidentiality from a trained volunteer who will not judge them or even give advice – but will *listen* to them. It can be a tremendous relief to voice your worries; often just bringing them into the open can make them bearable. Sharing problems can help to put them into perspective, and can help desperate people to live through another day, another week, another year.

During the Christmas period of 1990, 63,000 people phoned the Samaritans. That is why at least 7,000 Samaritan volunteers will be giving up some of their time during this period, many of whom will be on duty on Christmas Day itself.

Prayer

Let us think for a moment of those ordinary men and women, over 22,000 of them, who have trained as Samaritans and regularly give up their time, unpaid, to work at their local Samaritan branches. We give thanks for them especially at Christmastime, and for their dedication in offering a sympathetic ear to people whose misery drives them to desperate measures at this season when most of us are enjoying ourselves.

We pray that, in all our contacts with people at school and at home, we may be sensitive to people's inner suffering and give them the opportunity to talk about their worries and share their burdens before they become unbearable.

Amen

2 MIND

Use at least two readers, with a new voice for the passage about Henry.

MIND is the National Association for Mental Health. It is called MIND because this word has a variety of meanings. The mind is our mental capacity, but as a verb it tells us to 'mind' about people in distress, and to 'mind' them or take care of them.

MIND is a charity which helps people in any sort of mental distress. It might be the confusion brought on by Alzheimer's disease, or in old age by senility. Or it might be depression, which is becoming more and more common in our stressful lives. Mental illness is no longer something which happens to someone else. In the course of a year, one in four people will suffer from psychiatric symptoms of some sort. Intelligent, healthy and successful men, women and young people can be reduced to the point of mental exhaustion or breakdown. MIND advertises in doctor's surgeries, libraries and work-places, offering help to people who cannot cope any longer with their own emotional problems or with those of relatives whom they look after.

MIND has 250 local associations, some very large, some very small. They offer a variety of services which include day centres where people can go for counselling and practical help, sheltered housing, and various self-help groups. MIND also publishes a range of books and leaflets, and gives information on all aspects of mental health problems through telephone help lines and by letter.

For Christmas 1991, MIND sent out a Christmas card to all its supporters. But this card was not for them to keep. It was an unused card for them to write in their own message for the people who would be helped by this organisation at Christmas. MIND realised how important it was to keep their day-centres open over the Christmas period, including Christmas Day. The cards were shared out from their headquarters between all their centres, to go up as part of their decorations and to bring good wishes and messages of friendship and support to all the people in distress who would visit these centres at Christmastime.

Perhaps the best way to explain the value of these centres at Christmas is to tell you about Henry.

Henry is a widower and, now that his wife Audrey has died, he lives alone. Christmas had always been a very special time for Henry and Audrey, and after 10 years of happily married life, Henry couldn't bear the thought of spending Christmas all on his own. The thought of having no one to wrap presents for, having no one to pull a cracker with or drink a toast with on Christmas Day, and the idea of having to sit in the silence of his lonely room, whilst all the happy memories of Christmas past came flooding back, was more than he could face.

That's why he spent Christmas with MIND last year. Henry's local MIND centre organised a special Christmas lunch for everyone who visits the centre. It was a very special party with over 140 people tucking into turkey and all the trimmings, chatting away, singing songs, even playing a few party games. It was such a joy for Henry to spend time with others. He made many friends that day.

To Henry, the most important part of the whole day was the chance to meet others who knew just what he was going through, people who offered him friendship and support to help him through a difficult time. And as the centre is open all year round, Henry's become a regular visitor, spending time with his new found friends.

(*MIND newsletter, November, 1991*)

Prayer

I'd like you to spend a few moments imagining that you have been given a blank Christmas card to send to a local branch of MIND. What message would you like to send to the people, suffering from mental distress, who will read it?

3   The Salvation Army

One person should read the extract from the newsletter, another can introduce it and read the prayer.

The Salvation Army is well known for its social work as Salvationists go out into the community, easily recognised in their navy uniforms, helping the poor and needy.

At Christmastime, in the dead of winter, we probably think of their work among the single homeless. They provide over 50 hostels for the lucky ones, and do soup-runs to warm and nourish those who sleep rough on the streets of our big cities. At Christmas, their hostels provide Christmas dinner for such people.

A lot of their work also goes on unseen, with individuals and families in the communities that they serve. Here is an extract from a Christmas newsletter which was sent to their supporters:

Last Christmas morning a little girl was overwhelmed with joy to wake up and find that Father Christmas had left her the most wonderful present she'd ever seen – a big furry teddy bear to play with! For she'd never had a parcel to unwrap before, nor anything to call her own on this day of celebration . . . until you cared.

The letter goes on to tell the story of Debbie Mackinnon who had never before known the meaning of Christmas. She was one of the youngest children to enjoy a trip to Santa Claus Land, arranged by one of the Salvation Army Goodwill Centres (which are set up to befriend people in deprived inner city areas).

The youngsters, from one of the most deprived areas of Glasgow, could hardly believe their eyes as they were shown into Santa's grotto.

They each told Santa what they wanted for Christmas, until it was Debbie's turn. Asked what she'd like Santa to bring her on Christmas Eve, she fell silent, and no amount of encouragement could persuade her to utter a word. Eventually, 'Santa' coaxed her into explaining the reason for her shyness – she didn't know how to reply because she'd never been given a present before! Hugging Debbie, he told her that this year he would make sure to visit her.

Watching Debbie as she joyfully kissed Santa, the Salvation Army Major who'd organised the outing decided that somehow, this promise would be kept. Next day, inviting Debbie's mother for a cup of coffee at the Centre, he asked if the Army could help make Christmas a little more cheerful for their family. Mrs Mackinnon was delighted with his offer. Since her husband's redundancy – when Debbie was just a baby – the family were constantly struggling to make ends meet. 'We give her toys that are passed on to us,' she said, 'but she's never had something new to call her own.'

The Major was more than glad to arrange a little Christmas cheer for the family: not only food for a nourishing meal, but some clothes for Debbie – and a gaily wrapped parcel which Mrs Mackinnon hid until Christmas Day. I wish you could have seen Debbie's radiant face and the glad smiles of her parents as they watched her cuddle her beautiful new teddy on Christmas morning.

Prayer

This is a Christmas prayer that the Salvation Army sends out to its supporters, but it applies to anyone who shares with others at Christmastime.

> May the joy of sharing
> gladden the hearts of you and your loved ones
> at this holy time.

Amen

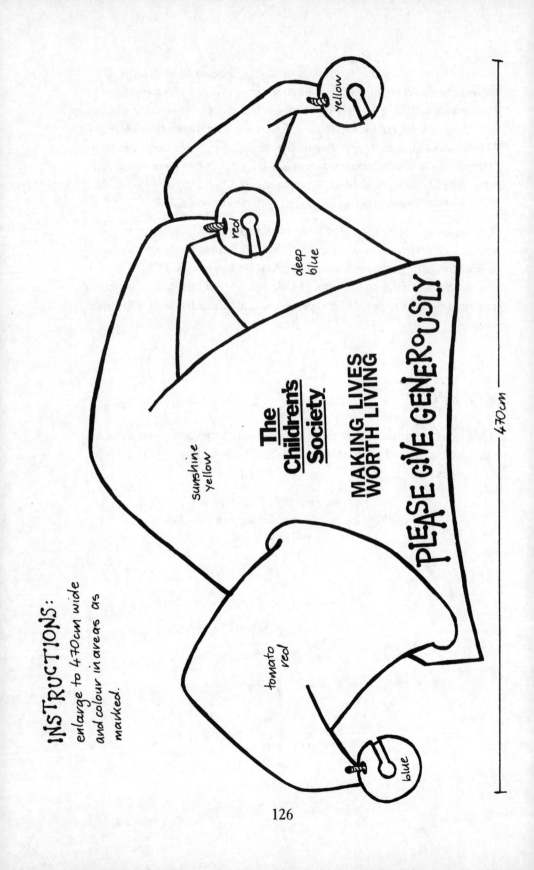

INSTRUCTIONS:
enlarge to 470cm wide
and colour in areas as
marked.

sunshine
yellow

tomato
red

deep
blue

red

yellow

blue

The
Children's
Society.

MAKING LIVES
WORTH LIVING

PLEASE GIVE GENEROUSLY

470cm

INDEX OF THEMES

DATES

January
31   World Leprosy Day

February
14   British Heart Foundation (i.e. St Valentine's Day heart)

Salvation Army door to door appeal

March
21   Marie Curie Cancer Care Daffodil Day

April
1   The Children's Society (i.e. April Fool's Day)

May
3rd week – Christian Aid Week
              MIND Week

last week – Samaritan Week

June
3rd week – Sight Savers Week

August
Salvation Army holidays

September
middle – Imperial Cancer Research Week

last Saturday – Age Concern (i.e. Grandparents' Day)

preceeding week – Age Concern Week

October
3rd week – Prisoner of Conscience Week (Amnesty International)

December
1   World AIDS Day

Christmas – RSPCA (i.e. 'Pets are not just for Christmas')

ADDRESSES

Age Concern England, National Council on Ageing
Astral House, 1268 London Road, London SW16 4ER
Tel. 081-679 8000

Amnesty International: British Section
93–119 Rosebery Avenue, London EC1R 4RE
Tel. 071-278 6000

British Heart Foundation. The heart research charity
14 Fitzhardinge Street, London W1H 4DH
Tel. 071-935 0185

Christian Aid
PO Box 100, London SE1 7RT
Tel. 071-620 4444

Ellenor Foundation
Livingstone Community Hospital, East Hill, Dartford, Kent DA1 1SA
Tel. 0322 221315

Friends of the Earth
26–28 Underwood Street, London N1 7JQ
Tel. 071-490 1555

Help the Aged
St James's Walk, London EC1R 0BE
Tel. 071-253 0253

Imperial Cancer Research Fund
PO Box No 123, Lincoln's Inn Fields, London WC2A 3PX
Tel. 071-242 0200

Isle of Wight Donkey Sanctuary
Betty Haunt Lane, Newport, Isle of Wight PO30 4HR
Tel. 0983 821593/520234

LEPRA The British Leprosy Relief Association
Fairfax House, Causton Road, Colchester, Essex CO1 1PU
Tel. 0206 562286

Marie Curie Memorial Foundation
28 Belgrave Square, London SW1X 8QG
Tel. 071-235 3325

MIND National Association for Mental Health
22 Harley Street, London W1N 2ED
Tel. 071-637 0741

Monkey World, Chimpanzee Rescue Centre
Longthornes, East Stoke, Wareham, Dorset BH20 6HH
Tel. 0929 462537

Royal Society for the Prevention of Cruelty to Animals
Causeway, Horsham, West Sussex RH12 1HG

Salvation Army
101 Queen Victoria Street, London EC4P 4EP
Tel. 071-329 0782

Samaritans
10 The Grove, Slough SL1 1QP
Tel. 0753 532713

Save the Children Fund
Mary Datchelor House
17 Grove Lane, Camberwell
London SE5 8RD
Tel. 071-703 5400

Shelter, The National Campaign for Homeless People
88 Old Street, London EC1V 9HU
Tel. 071-253 0202

Sight Savers, Royal Commonwealth Society for the Blind
PO Box 191, Haywards Heath, West Sussex RH16 1FN
Tel. 0444 412424

Spastics Society
12 Park Crescent, London W1N 4EQ
Tel. 071-636 5020

The Terrence Higgins Trust
52–54 Gray's Inn Road, London WC1X 8JU
Tel. 071-831 0330

United Nations Association UK
3 Whitehall Court, London SW1A 2EL
Tel. 071-930 2931/2

UNICEF UK
55 Lincoln's Inn Fields, London WC2A 3NB
Tel. 071-405 5592

Water Aid
1 Queen Anne's Gate, London SW1H 9BT
Tel. 071-233 4800